THE ILLUSIONS OF A NATION

Myth and history in the novels of F. Scott Fitzgerald

THE ILLUSIONS
OF A NATION

Myth and history in the novels
of F. Scott Fitzgerald

JOHN F. CALLAHAN

University of Illinois Press
Urbana Chicago London

To MICHAEL S. HARPER
in kinship

If in the old crystal
ball there are no images,
make them, pure and round,
and close to the heart.

Michael S. Harper

Preface

In 1968 Eugene McCarthy called those responsive to his presidential campaign a "constituency of conscience." In that context awareness became process; private reflections evolved into political action as citizens independently came to the same conclusion about power and policy in America. Unfortunately, the campaign bearing the name of Eugene McCarthy did not make up its mind about the limits of the existing political structure until the chance for power was gone. Illusions led to confusion between the people and their institutions of government. The truth about America has got to precede allegiance to any structure that has misrepresented history. This is particularly true in the year 1972.

A writer too has his constituency, a constituency of consciousness. For ten years Fitzgerald has been on my mind as a novelist who captured the complexity of the American idealist, the frailty of his historical and psychic awareness together with his "willingness of the heart." Fitzgerald's men express within their lives that national failure of contact between the individual and the institutional structures of his culture. My point of view on Fitzgerald as well as the context I have created around his novels depended for its reverberations on contact with friends.

The marrow of friends lies in their names:

Art Titus
Mike Hollington
Ben Barker-Benfield
Neil Kleinman
Dick Wasson
Ed Brandabur
Agnes Brandabur
Jerry Baum
Mort Jacobs
Robert and Elizabeth Michael
Jack and Diane Hart

Finally, I want to acknowledge the unique help of three persons: Michael Harper, to whom the book is dedicated and for whom much of it was written literally and metaphorically—"where are my pages?"; Sherman Paul, who, despite a two-year metaphor of silence on my part, enthusiastically and perceptively directed the dissertation from which this book developed; and, most lovingly, Susan Kirschner, now my wife, who guided me and the manuscript through difficult moments with sympathy, intelligence, and love.

Contents

THE ILLUSIONS OF A NATION

Myth and history in the novels of F. Scott Fitzgerald

one

The creation of an American mythos

1

History, myth, and personality together illuminate the vision of America embodied by F. Scott Fitzgerald in *The Great Gatsby*, *Tender Is the Night*, and *The Last Tycoon*. What, in America, have been the relationships between complex human personality, history, and those myths summoned to explain the facts of history? What in the national past tempts succeeding generations to evade their history and seek mythologies of fraudulent innocence? Particularly misleading, when applied to history, is the mythic mode's assumption that ongoing experience endlessly repeats past patterns of action and policy. Nevertheless, history and myth raise the same questions for America: how does history rationalized subvert personality? How have dominant myths swayed consciousness away from complexity and freedom? Why have fixity, stereotype, and a one-dimensional, denotative perception won out over fluidity, archetype, and personality in the round?

History's purpose is to articulate facts and consciousness as those things are united through action in the world. Myths often structure facts which in turn have derived their existence from attitudes buried in the psychology and history of a people. Consider the phenomena of race and racism. Certainly racism has to do with economic advantage and a fear of human diversity, of autonomous personality. In order to survive according to their preconceptions, the New England Puritans separated their culture from Indians who had lived with the land for thirty thousand years. To achieve the splendor of England's landed gentry, the Virginia-Carolina planters required at worst cheap labor, at best slavery. But this external, this economic, aristocratic motive connects to psychology. If decency, sympathy, and humaneness are values in a man's immediate society—family, friends, citizens —that man must justify his denial of others' humanity, particularly if he is prepared to institutionalize inhumanity through a slave system. In fact, justification becomes rationalization; but, to be successful, rationalization demands the creation of a myth as the final line of defense against those who would change the structure of culture and, therefore, the course and purpose of history. Specifically, the Southern master class and the Northern slave traders seized an emblem of racial difference—black skin— and created the myth of white supremacy in order to seal as a given of future history a course of action simply deemed necessary to profit and aristocracy during colonization. "Catch a nigger by the toe and if he hollers let him go." But the expectation is that he won't holler: first, because he is happy to be caught by the toe, and, second, because the speaker does not believe he is a human being. And if he should holler, his expression of discontent is considered an unwarranted threat against the country. By such processes do particular policies of injustice become absolute myths considered superior both to the changes of history and to the facts and integrity of personality.

What was in 1940 a confession of being for Fitzgerald has become in 1972 a categorical imperative for Americans. "I am interested," he wrote, "in the individual only in his relation to society." As if to aim his criticism at an idealist mode of perception, he added: "We have wandered in imaginary loneliness through imaginary woods for a hundred years—too long." [1] Cur-

---

[1] Fitzgerald's copy of *Dubliners*, *Fitzgerald Papers*, Princeton University Library.

rently, the situation permits no choice. Military technology, industrial wealth, and imperial policy have made America an empire toward the world, while institutional violence against man and nature threatens domestic society. Personalities necessarily are individuals "only in relation to society"—massive, central, reductive society. Even if one thinks of the moon and planets beyond as new frontiers of possibility, that very thrust into space confirms a linear, cut-and-run way of dealing with the world. If immediate realities are too pressing, too complex, then state, create, and capture another world. If history declares a past capital investment bankrupt, then float a new dream loan from the bank of American power with world resources as collateral. In America the dream seemed to relieve men from insecurity over identity and continuity. Reworked by Fitzgerald, the American dream became a mode of reality as well as a desire of personality. His novels trace the dream's origins to men's difficulty with history's paradox of finality and continuity, its objects to those sensual worlds promised in myth but denied by culture, its victims to idealists who could neither build upon nor change their history. If integrated, history, myth, and personality can embody a vision by which power and sensibility are transformed in this nation, a vision from which might follow a reconstruction whose value is not property but the integrity and diversity of personality.

2

An anatomy of American history requires three stages: the coming west to the new world and the response of Europeans to that world; the foundation of the republic and the nineteenth-century transition from republic to empire; and the full tide of empire in the twentieth century, the point of no return without full revision of consciousness and policy. But Americans have drawn back from the horrors of their history.

From the beginning those malcontents who sought to "civilize" the new world set in motion through the contradictory nature of their journey a schizophrenia from which American history and literature have been unable to escape. This divided reality they owed to the baggage they brought with them—a baggage of the mind. Colonials themselves, they fell back on a pragmatic and theoretical colonialism. Damned in the homeland, these Puritans aspired to election in America; others here, therefore, would be damned or there would have to be, as partially there would be in materialist Calvinist doctrine of the eighteenth century, a different vision. "For the problem of the New World was, as every new comer soon found out, an awkward one, on all sides the same: how to replace from the wild land, that which, at home they had scarcely known the Old World meant to them." [2] The past denied became a past enlarged, a past demanding loyalty in a vacuum of authority. Thus there developed little creative flow between these new white Americans as a society and the great and different continent they occupied and conquered. Their contact with the Indians—whom William Carlos Williams saw "as a natural expression of the place," "the flower of his world"—was essentially hypocritical. Not in the sense that there was conflict, bloodshed, and a transition of culture and institutions: these are facts of survival. But diversity was not tolerated. The new nation offered the Indian a choice between surrender and genocide. And genocide does not follow from external conditions; it follows from vision. Engaged in a fight for power, the colonists developed a grandiose euphemistic rationale that they might evade even the ordinary guilt of history. Rather than face survival's terms—you or me—they fell back on Calvinist modes—God or Satan, good or evil—to create and impose superiority: make America safe from the Indians.

From the start Americans, perhaps as a way of evading the guilt and madness which accompany history, have imposed

[2] William Carlos Williams, In the American Grain (New York: New Directions, 1956), p. 136.

values upon character and reality, and this arbitrarily. About the Indians and their place in America, Benjamin Franklin's quotation from an eighteenth-century orator followed by his own approving prophecy stands as an example and an indictment of election and damnation dogma in the eighteenth-century racial-cultural context: "The Great Spirit who made all things made everything for some *use*, and whatever *use* he designed anything for, that *use* it should always be put to. Now, when he made rum, he said 'LET THIS BE FOR INDIANS TO GET DRUNK WITH.' And it must be so. And indeed if it be the design of Providence to *extirpate* these *savages* in order to make room for the *cultivators of the earth*, it seems not improbable that rum may be the appointed means." (my italics).[3] Yet there were some of sensibility and aesthetic vision who saw this American superiority complex, this annihilation of otherness, as revelation of insecurity and that insecurity a revelation of the settlers' fear of a place with its own reality and presence, one unknown to them and their past. Indeed de Tocqueville's comments on genocide answer Franklin. They testify to the widespread symptoms of a racist and idealist psychology. In addition de Tocqueville's reflections demonstrate the continuity of America's relation to land and Indians from Franklin's mid-eighteenth-century observations to the expansionist period of the 1830's:

> That was the general sentiment. In the heart of this society, so policed, so prudish, so sententiously moral and virtuous, one encounters a complete insensibility, a sort of cold and implacable egoism when it's a question of the American indigenies. . . . This world belongs to us, add they. God, in denying its first inhabitants the faculty of civilizing themselves, has predestined them to inevitable destruction. The true proprietors of this continent are those who know how to take advantage of its riches.[4]

3 Max Farrand, ed., *The Autobiography of Benjamin Franklin* (Berkeley: University of California Press, 1949), p. 149.

4 Alexis de Tocqueville, "Fortnight in the Wilderness," in G. W. Pierson, ed., *Tocqueville in America* (New York: Peter Smith, 1938), p. 96.

Unable to wipe out their own past, these new Americans annihilate thirty thousand years of harmony between Indians and
America.

The "Robber Barons" and "Empire Builders" of a post-Civil
War America, reconstructed along aggressive materialist lines,
acted out de Tocqueville's analysis. According to Franklinian
doctrine (Calvinism distilled through Poor Richard), a man's
worth, or, if one prefers, God's election of man, is determined
and demonstrated by his material success. Thus, in actuality, the
Alger myth of the self-made man takes on a horrifying literal
meaning. Man was not a man until he had proven himself by
owning the world. In terms of identity one was no longer born
of woman into a society where one found purpose and a place.
Instead, one symbolically gave birth to himself by becoming
"worth his weight in gold." Material facts were their own justification. No matter how savagely fortunes were achieved, mere
possession of wealth and resources proved to Robber Barons that
it was right and just that they should own the world. Material-
ism, capitalist variety, finds its roots in the dogma of predestination. Possession of the world reflects election. As for the poor or
the damned: if God (or a history governed by Western systems)
has condemned them, it is not for the elected to save such creatures, whether Indians, Africans made slaves, or the poor of all
races in all countries:

> Indian Massacres
> Manifest Destiny
> The Man's the *Thing* or Fugitive Slave Laws
> Open Door Policy
> Remember the Maine All the Way to the Philippines
> Make the World Safe for Democracy
> Watts, Newark, Detroit, My Lai, Attica. . . .

What moral and aesthetic vision, therefore, developed for the
American of sensibility, as rebellion succeeded to republic—with

Bill of Rights all right, but for propertied whites—republic which bloated gradually into an empire ruthless toward the revolutions of its time? Clearly, the dominant male archetype in American literature and culture substitutes imaginative dominion for the material ownership of his business counterpart. Yet this man of sensibility, perhaps from horror of complicity, also denies history. Whatever happened "back somewhere" is over as far as he and his generation are concerned.

Late in his life, F. Scott Fitzgerald cautioned his daughter against the temptation to ignore or reject the burden of the past, individual and collective. "You speak of how good your generation is, but I think they share with every generation since the Civil War the sense of being somehow about to inherit the earth." [5] Referred to here is an idealist context of man creating himself and the world in his own particular image or fancied image: man and America, Adam and Eden, each outside time and circumstance. There is in the history of this archetype a terrible desire to wash one's hands and those of future generations of the crimes committed in the name of America's foundation. Consider the male lineage of our literature in the nineteenth century, where the myth of the self-made man became a model for ideal individuals:

Emerson's "plain old Adam, the simple genuine self against the whole world."

Whitman's "I" in Song of Myself naming all that lives in the American garden, engaging things, but later, America having been found and owned, searching like old man Columbus for the "Passage to India."

Cooper's Natty Bumppo: Adam as "hard, isolate, stoic and a killer." [6] Or, Natty Bumppo as first cop in the garden. Friendly cop, but cop. Indeed, first National Guardsman.

[5] Andrew Turnbull, ed., *The Letters of F. Scott Fitzgerald* (New York: Charles Scribner's Sons, 1963), p. 96.

[6] D. H. Lawrence, *Studies in Classic American Literature* (New York: Viking Press, 1923), p. 62.

Melville's Ahab: "grand old heart," that rare American father with authority, kingship, mastery but who destroys the very humanity from which these things flow.

Ishmael: surviving but lost son without wife or mother to mourn for him. Who *perceives* "that in all cases man must lower or at least shift his conceit of attainable felicity, not placing it anywhere in the intellect or the fancy but in the wife, the heart, the bed," but who, *having perceived* this, returns in dreams to his homosexual rite of squeezing sperm.[7]

Billy Budd: Adam as hermaphrodite whose stutter suggests an intact, preconscious Adam. Adam as martyr, not redeemer. Adam as society's victim. Military Society.

Huck Finn, who, to survive himself, must "light out for the territory ahead of the rest," away from women and society's continuities.[8]

James's eastward explorers who must choose *between* America and their humanity; mature personality, that is.

The same intactness, at once insulation and isolation, prevailed, according to William Carlos Williams's mythos, in those men who set the course of American history: "There has not appeared in the New World anyone with sufficient strength for the open assertion. So with Franklin, the tone is frightened and horribly smug—at his worst; it flames a little in DeSoto; it is necessary to Boone to lose himself in the wilds; there are no women—Houston's bride is frightened off; the New Englanders are the clever bone-men. Nowhere the open, free assertion save in the Indian: this is the quality." [9] The beginning of American history is that moment of apprehension which Fitzgerald presents in its original and subsequent form—Western man's first contact with America. Here, in art and in history, a unique moment in time mingles with the prototype of "all aspiration—not

[7] Herman Melville, *Moby-Dick or, the Whale* (New York: Hendricks House, 1952), p. 415. My italics.

[8] Mark Twain, *The Adventures of Huckleberry Finn* (New York: Harper and Brothers, 1912), p. 376.

[9] Williams, *In the American Grain*, pp. 154–55.

just the American dream but the human dream" [10]—the dream
of unity, integration, cohesion between mind and matter, man
and nature, the dream wherein one heightens the world and is
himself heightened by the world. Perhaps a universal aesthetic
could rescue history from a linear, merely chronological mode.
Fitzgerald's re-creation of collective, ancestral contact with America goes beyond the imposition of stereotype, particularly that
stereotype created to disguise the truth. Instead, at the end of
Gatsby we behold a historical as well as a mythic archetype.
Heeding the standard Ralph Ellison sets for archetype, we confront complexities of Western history in relation to those "abid-
ing patterns of human existence which underlie racial, cultural,
and religious differences." [11]

Two modes of time and human experience look out at us
from the last page of *The Great Gatsby*. There is the mythic
moment, what Fitzgerald, in *Tender Is the Night*, calls that
"lush mid-summer moment outside time" (175)—that moment
when experience is so overpowering that it seems to annihilate
time and space. Alongside, intervening to break the spell, is the
sense of any such moment as perishable and historical. Without
historical consciousness himself, Gatsby does not perceive the
dissipation of his dreams in the past. Neither does Carraway lift
the veil from those past circumstances which made the dream
illusory. Spatially, his allusions are vague: "somewhere back in
that vast obscurity beyond the city." Temporally, the process is
clarified by allusion to "the dark fields of the republic." [12] This
reference includes the westward push, "the right of our manifest
destiny to spread over this whole continent," [13] but also the Re-

10 Fitzgerald's remark is quoted by Andrew Turnbull in *Scott Fitzgerald*
(New York: Charles Scribner's Sons, 1962), p. 307.
11 Ralph Ellison, "A Very Stern Discipline," *Harper's* (March, 1967), p. 80.
12 F. Scott Fitzgerald, *The Great Gatsby* in *Three Novels* (New York:
Charles Scribner's Sons, 1925; reset, 1953), p. 137. Henceforth all references
from *The Great Gatsby*, *Tender Is the Night* and *The Last Tycoon* will refer
to the *Three Novels* edition and will appear in the text as page numbers.
13 Robert C. Winthrop, quoted in *Encyclopedia of American History*, ed.
Richard B. Morris (New York: Harper and Brothers, 1953), p. 193.

construction period in American history, and the turn-of-the-century transition from republic to empire. In any case, the time-space continuum of possibility ended early in the New World—as soon as America was charted, as soon as this continent was known and owned in the same gesture. What Carraway does not do is to make connections between moral and aesthetic failure in America and the character and policies of a social, economic, and political system.

In short, whether on behalf of creation or destruction, history and myth function together. In its totality *The Great Gatsby* sketches the evolution of America from "fresh green breast of the new world" to "valley of ashes," from continent with a spirit "commensurate to man's capacity for wonder" to place of nightmare, exhaustion, and death. Founded upon the myth of a new Eden, the history of the United States has displaced that vision into an industrial, excremental reality. The name given to matter in Fitzgerald's twentieth-century America, the "valley of ashes," suggests that the medium of creation is used up, burned out. Worse than that, the land itself has become a ghoulish creation: "—a fantastic farm where ashes grow like wheat into ridges and hills and grotesque gardens; where ashes take the forms of houses and chimneys and rising smoke and, finally, with a transcendent effort, of men who move dimly and already crumbling through powdery air" (19). In American scripture, *Genesis* celebrates the industrial-capitalist word become not flesh but refuse. The breath of creation is smoke which brings contamination to the land. Organic becomes inorganic; living things become corpses. In the prophetic terms of American geography and frontiers, we are witness to a spoiled Middle West in this eastern urban dumping ground. The wheat is not real wheat, but ashes and dust. The contemporary *genius loci* is no god of fertility, but Doctor T. J. Eckleburg, all eyes and no sight, impercipient Tiresias in billboard costume.

No wonder, then, that in this culture, personality, especially women, as well as America itself, becomes spoil to be plundered.

So that from the beginning even a Gatsby, who wishes to become a human being, falls victim to an unconscious correspondence between Daisy and the fruits of success which politicians and merchants (Benjamin Ben Franklin is dual prototype) allude to in their promise of the American dream. To Gatsby, Daisy, "gleaming like silver, safe and proud above the hot struggles of the poor," changes from woman to treasure (116–17). As woman, she is "perishable"; as silver or golden girl, an immortal. Precious metal becomes the only way of preserving the ideal; silver, as incorruptible metal, permanently objectifies the dream, the idea of success. Thus, dream becomes commodity, and to fulfill the dream, personality becomes mechanism.

3

Finally, this history was conceived, carried out, and justified in the crucible of American myth. Myth can illuminate phenomena of individual and collective experience, or it can impose arbitrary and false explanations on reality in order to disguise the nature of human experience and personality. I distinguish between myth as lie—whether consciously and deliberately invented or unconsciously accepted as part of one's culture and history—and myth as truth, when, to paraphrase Ralph Ellison, a transparent overlay is placed over the life of an individual or history in such a way that we are made to see ourselves in the round, with complexity. Myth as lie, as stereotype in the reductive mode, restricts possibility, freezes experience, denies freedom; whereas myth as truth, as archetype, with its modes of connotation and implication, suggests new arrangements of human essentials confirmed by past experience. Ellison's example brilliantly humanizes these points:

On the stage of Town Hall a few days before the 1964 Democratic Convention, a group from the Mississippi Freedom Democratic party talked of their experiences. To the facile eye one of the men who talked there might well have been mistaken

for the Sambo stereotype. He was Southern, rural; his speech
was heavily idiomatic, his tempo slow. A number of his surface
characteristics seemed to support the stereotype. But had you
accepted him as an incarnation of Sambo you would have missed
a very courageous man—a man who understood only too well
that his activities in aiding and protecting the young Northern
students working in the Freedom Movement placed his life in
constant contact with death, but who continued to act.[14]

Indeed, with this man there is the further complexity of stereotype camouflaging archetype in order to change the historical
system responsible for that very stereotype of black people. In
American literature and history there is little such *dynamic* complexity in the use of myth, little such unity and integration of
human needs, qualities, and strategies. Myths in America have
been schizophrenic, not actively polar; the axis has not turned;
each pole has stayed fixed, cut off from contact with its opposite.

The dominant idealist-materialist poles of the American myth
circuit yield up a common source in the opposite, yet complementary Puritan dogmas of Antinomianism and Arminianism.
The Antinomian conviction that ultimate being and power lay
in God as omnipresent, immanent, unchanging Spirit led to an
idealism, pervasive in American romanticism, that viewed reality
and experience as states removed from finite time, states existing
in the mind and/or the eternal kingdom of paradise. The Ar-
minians, with their denial of predestination and of the immediate, subjective experience of God, and their doctrine that man
earns, even demands, grace as reward for his works, are prophets
of Ben Franklin, Horatio Alger, John D. Rockefeller, and of the
self-made man psychology of success and of personality. On
parallel iron rails, each track runs to the same destination: an incapacity to respect the integrity of *other* things and *other* beings.
For aggression (owning, exploiting, annihilating the other person) and idealization (turning the other into an image within
the perceiver or lover's mind) both destroy personality.

[14] Ellison, "A Very Stern Discipline," p. 90.

Whether we consider an individual or a nation, personality and history are tested by their relationship to what is other in the world. In Fitzgerald, the metaphor for relationship is love, the dominant mode idealist; so it is necessary to keep in mind Freud's cautions about the denial of physical reality and the fact of difference: "At the height of being in love the boundary between ego and object threatens to melt away. Against all the evidence of his senses, a man who is in love declares that 'I' and 'you' are one, and is prepared to behave as if it were a fact." [15] To greater or lesser degree, love and personality provide Fitzgerald's idealists, Gatsby and Diver, a way into the timeless, the ideal world. In these novels the Adam and Eve myth becomes a fable of psychological idealism; Adam (Gatsby and Diver) creates Eve (Daisy and Nicole) from his own flesh, from his vision, while sleeping; woman becomes not herself, but dream realized. As they fall in love their "moral position" equals that of R. W. B. Lewis's new Adam who "was prior to experience, and in his very newness . . . fundamentally innocent. The world and history lay all before him." [16] But joined by women, real and imaginary, these idealists confront the structures and authorities of the world, a world which distinguishes between objects and image, fact and word, power and desire.

The alternative myth, the reality which idealists sought to escape, unveils the aggression beneath the rhetoric of democracy. This plunderer archetype possesses what D. H. Lawrence called the essential, unmelted American soul, the American male, isolate, beyond continuity and society, who finally "lives by death, by killing, but who is pure white." [17] Those whom official American History reveres as explorers, prototypes of civilization, owe a tithe to this tradition. One thinks of the Lewis and Clark expedition giving unnamed Indian women venereal disease and

[15] Sigmund Freud, *Civilization and Its Discontents*, trans. and ed. by James Strachey (New York: W. W. Norton, 1962), p. 13.

[16] R. W. B. Lewis, *The American Adam* (Chicago: The University of Chicago Press, 1955), p. 5.

[17] Lawrence, *Studies in Classic American Literature*, p. 63.

blind babies on the Oregon Trail, and of Buffalo Bill, whom Fitzgerald mythologizes in *Gatsby* as Dan Cody, "pioneer debauchee." Cody's medium is matter, not mind or imagination; his psychology, the satisfactions of plunder and accumulation; his moral aesthetic, the forms of violent subjugation. Unlike Marse Tom Buchanan, born into the leisure class and its Gilded-Age country-house barbarism, Cody lives and dies by brutality in the field—those blood "dark fields of the republic." Old with name and fame—in the real world there were several competitors for the right to be called Buffalo Bill—Dan Cody comes east, not like Daniel Boone to tell of the West's wild beauty and diversity; rather, miming his younger self, Cody panders to the worst instincts of the eastern seaboard, its desire to experience vicariously "the savage violence of the frontier brothel and saloon."

Dissenters within the American mythic tradition, sensualists with a gift for history like Williams and Lawrence, have exposed and rejected these idealist-materialist poles of American experience. They have replaced these schizophrenic visions with a myth of contact. Throughout *In the American Grain* William Carlos Williams puts most damning emphasis upon the failure of men and generations of men to contact sensuously and imaginatively the physical world, human and natural. Given American technology—recall, in Fitzgerald, Nicole Warren's metamorphosis at the end of *Tender Is the Night* to edifice, to metallic personality—Williams's most profound insight is his connection between the Puritans' refusal to touch the life around them and the twentieth century when the American aesthetic has become "the horrid beauty of its machines." [18] The world more and more verifies this perception of America as *deus ex machina*, its Adams as automatons. Perhaps, for example, the most remarkable thing about three national film versions of World War II (the Japanese *Fires on the Plain*, German *The Bridge*, and Polish *Ashes and Diamonds*) was that despite the wide diversity of the three films, the image of American soldiers as one-dimensional, me-

[18] Williams, *In the American Grain*, p. 68.

chanical men was identical in each. Yet Williams saw America as female, a woman different from our dreams, unique in her own right; a woman to be known through strength and tenderness, complexity and variety of response. To him, as D. H. Lawrence wrote in a little-known review of *In the American Grain*, America "is a myth-woman who will demand of men a sensitive awareness, a supreme sensuous delicacy, and at the same time an infinitely tempered resistance, a power of endurance and resistance." [19]

Here, *dynamic* polarity between contact and resistance, self and other, is essential to fruitful relationship with America, a historical and a mythic reality involving place and personality. Columbus and Boone in history, Gatsby in the novel, typify this approach to America. Serving the Spanish government that had outfitted his ships, Columbus, the individual, nevertheless responded to the challenge. He saw America as a new world on every level, but first and instinctively on the primary level of physical characteristics. The originality of his diary rests on the consuming wonder expressed at the difference between America's natives and trees and everything else in his experience: "They are themselves neither black nor white. . . . Their legs are very straight, all in one line and no belly. . . . I saw many trees very unlike those of our country. Branches growing in different ways and all from one trunk; one twig is one form and another is a different shape and *so unlike that it is the greatest wonder in the world to see the diversity.*" [20] Difference and otherness give integrity to being and inspire admiration and reverence from Columbus. Of course these very qualities betray him to history's greed. Spain sends conquistadores in his place. De Leon, Cortez: intimidate the Indians' spirit; ship their gold, their civilization—"of hammered gold and gold enameling" [21]—

[19] D. H. Lawrence, "American Heroes," a review of William Carlos Williams, *In the American Grain*, in *Nation*, vol 112, no. 3171 (April 14, 1926), p. 413.
[20] Williams, *In the American Grain*, p. 26.
[21] W. B. Yeats, "Sailing to Byzantium," *Collected Poems of W. B. Yeats* (New York: Macmillian, 1956), p. 192.

back to Christian Spain. Immediately, history murders sensibility.

Another Williams hero, Daniel Boone, contemporary of George Washington, extends the myth of contact as the first white man to explore Kentucky. Like Columbus his possession of the land is aesthetic: "And among all the colonists like an Indian, the ecstacy of complete possession of the new country was his alone! In Kentucky he would stand, a lineal descendant of Columbus on the beach at Santo Domingo, walking up and down with eager eyes while his men were gathering water." [22] Like Columbus he would grow bitter, not at Indians who killed his eldest son, but at " 'those damned Yankees,' who took from him, by the chicanery of the law and in his old age, every last acre of the then prosperous homestead he had at last won for himself after years of battle in the new country." [23] Unlike Columbus, who pined away in moody European penury, Boone, "once more a wanderer," "struck out through Tennessee for 'more elbow-room,' determined to leave the young nation which he had helped establish, definitely behind him." [24] Once again, history forces the man who would discover and love America into an unreal, unhealthy choice. The land or society: choose one; woman or the Indian: choose only one. Fitzgerald's Dick Diver belongs at the extreme ironic end of these brothers who in maturity leave family and society to wander through unviolated regions of America; such men discover and contact America in a completely male context without wife or children or sense of ancestry.[25] Paradoxically, penetration of America, physical and aesthetic, seems to cut off men from human continuities.

With Gatsby, Fitzgerald changes the relation between Amer-

[22] Williams, *In the American Grain*, pp. 136–37.
[23] *Ibid.*, p. 139.
[24] *Ibid.*
[25] It may be that the isolations of the frontier are simply extensions of the American social world. That is, men in business or in political or professional life may have been and may be just as isolated from women and complexity of experience as those who were literally isolated on the frontier.

ica and woman from deductive to inductive mode. Gatsby's discovery of America is revealed by his passionate tenderness toward Daisy. The ladder of desire begins at the earth, with the body:

> Those masterful images because complete
> Grew in pure mind, but out of what began?
> A mound of refuse or the sweepings of the street
> Old kettles, old bones, old rags, that raving slut
> Who keeps the till. Now that my ladder's gone,
> I must lie down where all the ladders start,
> In the foul rag-and-bone shop of the heart.[26]

Consider Yeats's metaphor of the ladder and personality as Carraway describes, in Gatsby's language, the incarnation with Daisy:

> Out of the corner of his eye Gatsby saw that the blocks of the sidewalk really formed a ladder and mounted to a secret place above the trees—he could climb to it, if he climbed alone, and once there he could suck on the pap of life, gulp down the incomparable milk of wonder.
>
> His heart beat faster and faster as Daisy's white face came up to his own. He knew that when he kissed this girl, and forever wed his unutterable visions to her perishable breath, his mind would never romp again like the mind of God. So he waited, listening for a moment longer to the tuning fork that had been struck upon a star. Then he kissed her. At his lips touch she blossomed for him like a flower and the incarnation was complete (84).

"Unutterable visions" and "perishable breath." There is a clear polarity between *ideal* world, with its isolating imaginative dimension, and *bodily* world, with its recognition of otherness. Gatsby forsakes the ladder, the "pure mind" of "masterful images," for the girl. Unlike the "Dutch sailors," Gatsby does not simply look; he touches. Daisy, in the beginning, is not Gats-

[26] Yeats, "The Circus Animals' Desertion," *Collected Poems*, p. 336.

by's rib, but a different person. She blossoms for Gatsby *after* he kisses her. The "unutterable visions" for which Gatsby is tempted to reach have become embodied through sexuality. There is also the suggestion of Gatsby as Adam creating Daisy as his Eve, yet the circumstance which makes woman real to man is sexual and bodily.

Gatsby, son of Cody, who would take "what he could get, ravenously and unscrupulously" from Daisy—Gatsby, plunderer, becomes Gatsby, discoverer. He becomes a human being and briefly—their October month of love commemorates Columbus —humanizes Daisy. Their short time of love is long enough for them to establish a rapport based not on words or any single act of love but upon harmony of physical presence. Bodily contact becomes one with rhythm of consciousness. Gatsby and Daisy simply *are*, one to the other. Myth and personality harmonize the same theme: one's deepest context must be other human beings.

Here too, history and society intervene. Gatsby must leave for the war, breaking that continuity of relationship which might allow Daisy to remain a woman instead of becoming his dream image. Soon she becomes debutante participant in the failure of memory so typical in America. As time passes, circumstance proves stronger for her than memory of experience. Under stress, Daisy is the property of class and background. Her parents "effectually prevented" her from joining Lieutenant Jay Gatsby in New York. Her rhythm no longer is herself, but that imposed by leisure-class social seasons. We must remember, too, that Daisy's world and the American world generally are not natural or necessary realities but ones imposed arbitrarily on personality.

According to the novel's drama, love and personality (contact) are contained within society and history. Gatsby's very universal qualities, his "heightened sensitivity," make it impossible for him to strike through the American system. Beauty in America belongs to those who can afford to protect it against contingency and contact. Love becomes a commodity even for the idealist, because he, like Gatsby, will have to wed the dream's vision to something material, and in America everything of value can be bought. All matter is easily converted to currency of one form or another. Even Daisy. But, more destructively, even Gatsby. Without Daisy, he is nothing; he is as worthless as the bonds passed illegally over the counter of his Chicago "drugstore" after his death. The murder only externalizes what has already been internalized within Gatsby. For idealists, as Fitzgerald said, "There are no second acts in American lives." [27] After the first love, there is no other.

Columbus, Boone, Gatsby, and all their mythical brothers in the struggle to contact America raise, in their failure, an ultimate question about the efficacy of myth in relation to history. Are these discoverers, like Icarus, flying beyond the bounds of personality's very nature? Or is the American tragedy the responsibility of particular historical visions, the premises of Calvinism, say, or of that rationalism which gives the mind final authority over life? Narrator Carraway reflects on these issues in his stop-action vision of America at the novel's end: "And as the moon rose higher the inessential houses began to melt away until gradually I became aware of the old island here that flowered once for Dutch sailor's eyes—a fresh green breast of the new world. Its vanished trees, the trees that had made way for Gatsby's house, had once pandered in whispers to the last and greatest of all human dreams" (137). Subtly, Carraway's description of the first Western encounter with the new world relies on his own Puritan-platonic heritage. Western man, from idealism, won't grant America beauty and existence apart from his own mind; in itself, the world is tainted. Nature—recall the medieval woman-body, man-spirit duality—panders to the male imagination, promises falsely to embody what, according to Carraway's perception, can never be realized by matter in time outside the

[27] Fitzgerald, *The Last Tycoon*, p. 163.

Cartesian chambers of the mind. For Carraway the doctrine of original sin has turned into an aesthetic as well as a historical mechanism.

But in America the values of Carraway's coordinates, perceiver and aesthetic object, have been reversed by history. Four hundred years ago there was the American continent, its being, its beauty intact, almost waiting for the new element—Western man. For it was not, as Carraway claims, "man," generally and universally, who at that stage beheld the new world. Even if one accepts his context, the "Dutch sailor's eyes" (seen as at once ravished and ravishing) did not undo the American continent. Presumably their vision and Gatsby's dream are not foreign or impossible to human personality. No, the Dutch sailors are to blame as men imprisoned in a particular, mercantile-historical context. Not for man, but for commercial man, expansionist man embarked already on a new industrial technology, was "aesthetic contemplation" undesired, uncomprehended, nothing more than a moment of wonder outside the motion of time and circumstance.

Unrequested, this moment immediately dissolved. Unprepared for, it was forgotten. Idealism realized through acquisition; admire the trees, then step back into history and cut them down. The same conditions that abort love, spur on empire.

In the novel, however, both Gatsby and Carraway lack any sense of history's paradox, the sense that history is both final and ongoing. With Gatsby nothing was final, irrespective of actions and circumstances, so long as the dream engaged his heart. The past remained open to perfection; events could not end. His re-enactment of past interlude in another time, another place, and other circumstances—this and his death compose a text for our instruction: to repeat a pattern is not to understand the complexities and limitations of that pattern. Carraway, on the other hand, recognizes history as patterned events but believes that once an original event does happen, not only is *its* possibility annihilated, but present and future men shall repeat inevitably and endlessly the pattern of primal failure. Thus human choice and conduct become exhausted in advance of future act and experience. For scapegoat, platonic Calvinist Carraway chooses not history but reality itself. In *his* book, it was the myth itself, the dream of contact, that brought about man's fall. Not history and its systems but nature and personality themselves corrupted Carraway's primal America.

4

The myths of history as dream and as nightmare may be far apart, but the closed form of both tends to belittle present action and let men off the hook of their own decisions and experience. Consider again R. W. B. Lewis's American Adam, this time his conception of the innocent and intact Adam's double: that fallen, torturingly self-conscious, despairing Adam. According to Lewis, in such a man "skepticism takes the form of a hostility to human nature as self-wounded and self-wounding beyond repair; something which began as a valuable corrective to the claim of innocence in America and which has declined into a cult of original sin." [28] What Lewis alludes to is the world vision which descends upon a new Adam whose perspective of innocence and possibility turns, after experience of evil and of history's obstacles (nature's too), into an equally absolute viewpoint of pessimism and enclosure in a more and more masculine and ideological universe.

In perceptual and psychological terms what happens to would-be romantic heroes like Gatsby, Dick Diver, and the rationalist, Monroe Stahr, is not integration between pleasure and survival, but an unresolved, destructive conflict. Neither individual can unite his erotic-imaginative impulses to the painful, practical realities of a material and temporal framework. Almost at the moment he heightened his own and Daisy's identity through love, Gatsby discovered that she began to imprison his

[28] Lewis, *The American Adam*, p. 198.

being in a sheerly material, abstract world, a world that finally became "material without being real," a world of nauseous horror. Or consider Dick Diver's bind. Already twenty-eight, he rejects the repression of trying to satisfy his imaginative-erotic desires through the medium of his psychiatric profession; instead he chooses Nicole. But, given her history, this choice is itself an act of idealization, and Diver has only to be swallowed up by the very woman his imagination had desired to heighten and fulfill. But the chickens hidden away in "that foul rag-and-bone shop" of Diver's heart come home to roost. At bottom a schizophrenic, he is destroyed by those very facts and desires his mind believed it could circumvent in a God-like act of creation, i.e., his yielding to the wish that Nicole be "just a girl lost with no address save the night from which she had come" (26)—a wish, in other words, that she and America become magically unviolated. Here again, now in Diver's round complexity, stands Fitzgerald's theme: the failure of the American idealist either to integrate himself with or change the course of American history.

The charge to living personality is a clear imperative. To break free from the continuing death grip of our history, we must learn to face the facts and myths of our past. Believing that before an American could awaken from the nightmare of his past he must first understand the meaning of his dreams, novelist Fitzgerald does for the reader what Norman Brown claims psychoanalytic therapy does for the neurotic individual: "And the method of psychoanalytic therapy is to deepen the historical consciousness of the individual ('fill up the memory gaps') till he awakens from his own history as from a nightmare." [29] Illusion, gentility, euphemism: perhaps these are the coats which we, as well as Dick Diver, wear to cover up the horror of exploitation, of the American "heart of darkness." Fitzgerald's metaphorical account of American history and its system of thought and policy is not, in itself, an individual or historical solution. His archetypes do

[29] Norman O. Brown, *Life against Death: The Psychoanalytic Meaning of History* (Middletown, Conn.: Wesleyan University Press, 1959), p. 19.

show, however, how the ghosts of the past, unexposed, make ghosts of living men.

In his very refusal to let any light flicker at the tunnel's end in *Gatsby* and *Tender Is the Night*, Fitzgerald faces unflinchingly a truth about consciousness, frightening to those of us still searching for a way out, but a truth nevertheless. It is as if personality has its own unalterable laws so that if one, like Ishmael or Ahab, or Carraway, Diver, or Stahr in the novel, or President Lyndon Johnson in American foreign policy, understands his psychological and historical dilemma *after* a certain point, perception will be incapable of leading him to change his course. Even if there is a willingness to alter one's condition, the wiring between perception and kinetic impulse has frayed to a point of disconnection. Such loss of freedom, such *identification* with the objects of one's horror, is fatal both to change and to dynamic continuity.

The beginnings of a constructive polarity between self and reality struggle toward the light in Fitzgerald's alternative to his own "crack-up" identifications: "It was dangerous mist. When Wordsworth decided that 'there had passed away a glory from the earth,' he felt no compulsion to pass away with it, and the Fiery Particle Keats never ceased his struggle against t.b. nor in his last moments relinquished his hope of being among the English poets." [30] Vital to this creative flow between perception and action is a commitment to that negative capability which Keats defined as the perceptual and psychic circumstance "when man is capable of being in uncertainties, Mysteries, doubts, without any irritable reaching after fact or reason." [31] This capacity to hold constant one's identity at the same time that one sees other realities as contingent, changing, and uncertain is a notion reworked by Fitzgerald during his own period of personal and cos-

[30] F. Scott Fitzgerald, *The Crack-Up*, ed. Edmund Wilson (New York: New Directions, 1945), p. 81.

[31] Letter to George and Thomas Keats, December 21, 1817, in Hyde Edward Rollins, ed., *The Letters of John Keats*, 1814–21, vol. 1 (Cambridge: Harvard University Press, 1958), p. 193.

mic uncertainty. "The test of a first rate intelligence," he writes in "The Crack-Up" essay, "is the ability to hold two opposed ideas in the mind at the same time and still retain the ability to function." His illustration is moral in the deepest sense of individual and historical situations in America. "One should, for example," he concludes, "be able to see that things are hopeless and yet be determined to make them otherwise." [32]

If this statement represents an aesthetic categorical imperative for the novel, it also explains the novelist's own "confession of faith" to his daughter: "I guess I am too much a moralist at heart and really want to preach at people in some acceptable form rather than to entertain them." [33] After the fact, it comes close to being a perfect description of what Fitzgerald was trying to do in *Gatsby* and in *Tender Is the Night*. Specifically, he creates a series of contexts, each dependent upon contingent, though far-reaching, conditions of experience. So Carraway's and Diver's visions of history and personality should not be taken as absolutes, final and fixed, but as versions of reality that proceed from particular backgrounds, experiences, and perceptions. Such novelistic techniques of context and contingency compel us, for example, to regard point of view as often distinct in the different books of *Tender Is the Night*, dependent upon the stage its characters move across. Likewise we should see novelist Fitzgerald as a composite of different narrative modes: biographer-historian; movie camera; Rosemary's movie star's eyes; Nicole's hardening consciousness; impersonal chronicler; voice of the newsreel or of time itself; and mere recorder, without interpretation, of objects and gestures.

Finally, the issue, formal and otherwise, in Fitzgerald's and in all novels, is the issue of freedom: the achievement of integrity and diversity. For author and for reader it should be the essence of critical morality that a novel's world does exist. Not independently of other beings—for without consciousness a book as well

[32] Fitzgerald, *The Crack-Up*, p. 69.
[33] Turnbull, ed., *Letters of F. Scott Fitzgerald*, p. 63.

as a person is "material without being real"—but independently of our little set of perceptions. This is a novel's freedom.

Certainly, in America freedom demands liberation. Once again the old names: history, myth, personality. Through forms that are humanely passionate these things must change disintegration to cohesion, isolation to community. Or, as an angrier man, black poet Michael Harper, has written in his poem, "American History":

> Those four black girls blown up
> in that Alabama church
> remind me of five hundred
> middle passage blacks,
> in a net under water
> in Charleston harbor
> so *redcoats* wouldn't find them.
> Can't find what you can't see
> can you? [34]

The first act of liberation is to destroy one's cage.

[34] Michael S. Harper, *Dear John, Dear Coltrane* (Pittsburgh: University of Pittsburgh Press, 1970), p. 56.

two

A form beyond myth:
The rescue of history in
The Great Gatsby

I have left Act I for involution
and Act II. There mired in complexity,
I cannot write Act III.[1]

1

Implicit a form and a chronology: first the question; then its angles and complexities; finally, an action that resolves the drama. But explicit in Eugene McCarthy's "Lament for an Aging Politician" is the acknowledgment of an unspanned distance between consciousness and history. McCarthy's poem conveys the sense, going back to Oedipus, that perception is a curse, that the reward for seeing is punishment, usually in the form of paralysis. The poem shares with many first-person modern novels the further hint that complexity of form leads to paralysis of personal and historical wills. In other words, there can be a conflict between modern perceptual modes and the historian's responsibility to find causes for particular events. For instance, when applied to history, the impressionist notion that consciousness operates nonchronologically—that is, backwards and forwards over the past—may obliterate legitimate claims of respon-

[1] Eugene J. McCarthy, *And Time Began*, private edition (New York, 1968), p. 11.

sibility and causality from human actions. Constructively, temporal-perceptual arrangements which deny chronology and causality open up new perspectives because they expose the assumptions of chronology and causality as exactly that—assumptions, possible explanations for phenomena but explanations neither absolute nor necessary. Novelists like Fitzgerald and Conrad who would become moral historians must recognize the necessity for distance between a novel's outermost frame and the narrower perspective of the narrator. I say necessity because, without such a wide-angle lens, a given novel may fall prey to its narrator's vision of man and history as universally decided once and for all.

There is, to return to examples, a critical difference between McCarthy's persona and, say, Carraway and Marlow in *Gatsby* and *Heart of Darkness.* For McCarthy's aging politician does indeed lament; that is, he admits regretfully his own incapacity to change history, "to write Act III." At the same time he gives his audience the impression that modes of action can bring about new arrangements in the historical process. Contrast this with Marlow and Carraway. Marlow, the practical liberal, admires Kurtz's direct confrontation and involvement with evil, but he lies to the dead man's fiancee even though he knows this perpetuates the very idealism which destroys exploited and exploiter both. Likewise, Carraway, having re-created an experience through dislocations of time and relative points of view, universalizes all human history in a platonic-Calvinist fable. Recall his coda to *The Great Gatsby:* "So we beat on, boats against the current, borne back ceaselessly into the past" (137). No matter how well a man may swim, history's current pulls him backward. Not just he but we, individually and as a nation, will repeat the same cycle of dream and nightmare, ahistorical wonder and historical rape, which lay behind past and present experience in the novel. He, and he assumes we, will make no attempt to change society; experience has horrified Carraway into myth. History, he insists, is over.

Now there *are* universals in *The Great Gatsby*. These patterns have to do not only with nature and the seasons, but with the ongoing predicament of American culture and imagination. But universals like the novel's alliance among dream, money, accumulation, and holocaust do not arise in any predetermined, *a priori* mode. They form the given conditions in America because of particular, even unique values and events. So that if Gatsby's dream and "the service of a vast, vulgar, and meretricious beauty" (75) have become one and the same thing, it is because he has accepted, unconsciously or not, cultural premises which lead to no other conclusion. Carraway's skepticism follows from a related narrowness. Because one particular and general dream premise has evolved a grotesque and ugly conclusion, he throws out all syllogisms, all other configurations, as if Gatsby's first premise was, is, and shall be the only one possible for America.

But to repeat Gatsby's American cycle, as Carraway holds we are bound to do, seems in view of the novel's relative form a contingent proposition rather than a predetermined fact. In any case the question which must resolve historical, psychological, and moral issues in *The Great Gatsby* is the question of form. What, in Fitzgerald's view, is the effect of aesthetics on experience? Is Fitzgerald one with Carraway and his *Dunciad*-like prophecy that "universal Darkness buries All" in America? Or must we grant him, as we do Conrad in *Heart of Darkness* and Hemingway in *The Sun Also Rises*, the artist's "cold eye," that impersonality or negative capability which separates him from the vision, if not always the consciousness, of his narrator? I think we must. I think, too, that the reason critics deny Fitzgerald this critical faculty has to do more with his novelistic powers of sympathy than with his seductive triumvirate: life, legend, and confessions. In *Gatsby*, then, I think Fitzgerald uses his participant-narrator to make the living see the relationship between misapprehension of American history's facts and ideas and resignation to more of the same failure. Whatever the finalities within the novel, its contextual structure speaks of different possibilities for ongoing life and history in the world beyond.

Specifically, Fitzgerald so thoroughly particularizes Carraway and the middle-class stolidity and security of his background and values that we must beware of accepting his generalizations as God-like. All that is required of novelist Fitzgerald is that they be inevitably true to Carraway. Flexibility on the matter of point of view is necessary if one is to avoid saying yes or no to the historical vision expressed by Carraway in *Gatsby*. Rather than dismiss that vision as irrelevant or charge Fitzgerald with complicity in it, I prefer to call it a vision Fitzgerald chose for Carraway, given his particular social, economic, and psychological context.

Contextual form in *Gatsby* proceeds contrapuntally. One melodic theme becomes dominant because of reinforcement by variations modulated to other keys. The percussive effects of Buchanan's voice and the strings that follow Gatsby's story, these melodic lines complicate and intensify the oboes, say, which mark Carraway's journey and return in the novel. For purposes of form, the pivotal context has got to be Carraway's middle-class background, the role of his ancestors in American history, and his application of those values to the experience under scrutiny. Essential as a minor theme is the Buchanan context, particularly Tom's role as leisure-class plantation owner come north in the twentieth century. Finally, played out with great complexity is Gatsby's lower-class past (literal and mythic, for he has many fathers). The actual sire is Henry C. Gatz, "from a town in Minnesota," who, himself poor and ineffectual, lives by admiration of the American empire's power and wealth. More important are the historical-mythic forebears: those anonymous Dutch sailors; father-substitute Dan Cody who resembles in history Hopalong Cassidy; James J. Hill, who does the same service for Franklin's Poor Richard; and, most contemporarily, the gangster baron Wolfsheim, the immigrant Jew whose middle passage to American business is made through the rackets.

But Carraway, because he is narrator, calls the tune. His establishment, *before* he narrates the experience, of middle-class moral and social norms, reveals the commitments behind his vision of American history. Carraway may be the prodigal son, but, once returned home, this prodigal makes amends for his journey by an even stricter defense of ancestral values than is found in family gospel. It's as if Nick has internalized Gatsby. They, he thinks of the world's forces, will get me too if I don't retreat into the domestic and national cocoon: the middle western provinces.

2

We must, after all is said, begin at the beginning of *Gatsby* with its narrator's self-history. Carraway's preface (or really afterword to the novel) becomes for us, because it precedes the narrative, what the elder Carraway's advice had been to his son: a moral guide to the narrative itself. In form and tone the opening paragraphs resemble Franklin's *Autobiography* with its technique of having the teacher call attention to his mistakes before he stakes out more workable modes of conduct: "In my younger and more vulnerable years my father gave me some advice that I've been turning over in my mind ever since.

'Whenever you feel like criticizing any one,' he told me, 'just remember that all the people in the world haven't had the advantages that you've had.'" (3). Unlike Gatsby, Carraway gets instruction from his father about the middle class in a democracy. Furthermore, the advice is vague enough to allow the son several different interpretations. It suggests privilege of environment; it further urges relative perspectives of judgment, a graduated scale of moral taxation or accountability, notwithstanding the smugness in which it is couched.

Carraway, as he tells us freely enough, has used this formula to handle eccentric personalities. Until he meets Gatsby, "advantages" seem to mean personal qualities like proportion, stability, discipline, and taste. However, Nick soon introduces a restrictive provision: "Reserving judgments is a matter of infinite hope. I am still afraid of missing something if I forget that, as my father snobbishly suggested, and I snobbishly repeat, a sense of the fundamental decencies is parcelled out unequally at birth" (3). Here the hope of man re-creating himself collides with the determinist view of personality and history, the Calvinist principle of predestination, of man as damned or elected previous to his own consciousness. As narrator in *Gatsby*, Nick comes to see the collective "we" of America damned from the start. Not only is history already acted and written, finalized, but we are doomed to repeat its pattern in our lives even if individual minds and hearts resist its course. Past history has taken away *our* freedom. Carraway's context has become one's moral relation to others and to society. "Fundamental decencies": the simple view is that one receives them or not at birth. So we've got superiority based on both environment and on heredity.

What Carraway justifies is his decision to "come back home" (134). No longer will he reserve judgment. The complexities behind conduct no longer concern him; puritanically, he insists that the "world be in uniform and at a sort of moral attention forever" (3). One suspects that what Carraway seeks most to avoid are the total disillusionment and skepticism which have followed his journey to experience. Yet his categorical, official morality does not here lead to a neoclassical Eliotic (Babbitt, Eliot, Hulme) rejection of the romantic impulse.

Consider his reaction to Gatsby's fall. "Only Gatsby, the man who gives his name to this book," the man also whose uncritical nature, "appalling sentimentality," and willingness to traffic with corruption in pursuit of his dream, represented "everything for which I have an unaffected scorn"; only this man, Nick tells us solemnly, "was exempt from my reaction" (3). What Nick values in Gatsby are qualities he himself lacks: spontaneity; sensitivity outward; and, finally, that capacity for hope crushed in Carraway by the burden of history. His elegy for Gatsby at best oversimplifies, at worst distorts, the meaning of Gatsby's life: "No—Gatsby turned out all right at the end; it is what preyed on Gatsby, what foul dust floated in the wake of his dreams that temporarily closed out my interest in the abortive sorrows and short-winded elations of men" (4). What Carraway has done is abstract Gatsby from American culture. Yet what is great about Gatsby is his willingness as an idealist to "wed his unutterable visions to her perishable breath" (80), his willingness to connect with the culture. Even though it is other than his conceptual dream of reality, even though it is perishable, physical, Gatsby has thrown in his lot with the world. Now it is true, as Carraway claims, that "foul dust"—corruptions of culture and personality, aggressive ownership; lack of sensibility—"preyed on Gatsby." But in his way Gatsby prayed to, supplicated actively the shabbiness and corruption of that same culture. He was ultimately responsible for, if unconscious of, his complicity with the ravishing American nightmare.

Why then does the novel's witness, jury, and judge have his Gatsby pure and distinct from the world, a stance one feels Gatsby himself would not dare to take? He does, after all, look more than once "as if he had killed a man" (102). The answer lies within Carraway's ambivalent commitment to that middle-class, middle-western world of his adolescence and his ancestors.

"Clan, line, generations, traditions." These words confirm Carraway's continuous heritage. Far from being the "shiftless and unsuccessful farm people" (74) who are Gatsby's parents, the Carraway family formed the backbone of America. Like Gatsby, the Carraway clan indulges in romantic fantasies about itself—not, however, at the expense of a solid, everyday place in American society. On the contrary, their particular fantasy complements the economic and social position they enjoy. The tradition referred to is descent from the Scottish Dukes of Buccleugh, a *legend* with aristocratic pretensions, despite the *fact* of these Dukes as usurpers and plunderers. As if to acknowledge the truth beneath the legend, the Carraways in their American past have been careful to establish ownership, material security, and above all legitimacy—those realities most likely to survive fickleness, whether of time, circumstance, or imagination. But such middle-class legitimacy got its start only because the "founder of the line" (4) seized on the American equivalence between money and person. He "sent a substitute to the Civil War" (4). He used money to make money, *at the expense of some "unknown" other person.*

If the Civil War was a business deal to Nick's "hardboiled" great uncle, whom he is "supposed to look like" (4), World War I was for third-generation Nick a "counter-raid," as he calls America's role. The word both harks back to the Dukes of Buccleugh and, in its adolescent, history-as-adventure tone, sets the stage for Nick's journey East. For it is not as if he strikes out on his own, a pioneer. The family council before his departure indicates the degree of home-town control even over his intention to come East permanently. Thus, the provincial comes to the city not from any simple gesture of rebellion, but as an ambassador of family traditions and values.

3

Carraway's personality and its contextual value system emerge most definitely in his relationship with Jordan Baker. Insofar as sexual relationships reveal a cultural milieu, Nick's relationship parallels Gatsby's with Daisy. The difference consists in Carraway's lack of imaginative intensity and in his incapacity to integrate perspectives of class, morality, manners, and chronology, to see events and relationships going through aesthetic changes. Again ambivalence is the keynote. On the one hand Nick would like to join society, but on the other what is freedom to Jordan and to the Buchanans is irresponsible license according to the Carraway almanac.

The encounter reflecting these things ends Chapter Three, aptly the last chronological, single-viewpoint chapter. (Nick has been pursuing his education: of economics and sexuality. Presumably, his affair with the girl in the bond office's accounting department, and his decision to "let it blow quietly away," link him not only to Buchanan but also to the young Gatsby, in any case to the attitude that women are spoil from whom a man takes "what he can get" without tenderness or sensibility.)

Even more important here is Carraway's ongoing perspective of both outsider and insider. Before he narrows the lens to Jordan Baker, he tells what it felt like to stand outside New York's romantic social world. Although the scene he directs for us is not the mythic, last-man-having-lost-the-last-woman pilgrimage that Gatsby makes to Louisville after Daisy's marriage, it does show the same magnetic pull on the outsider of society's rhythm and mystery. Evenings, Nick does his lessons in the Yale Club's library, but "early to bed, early to rise" does not bury the desire for love and immediate contact with the social world which love seems to include in Fitzgerald. Always the lover is an actor performing "an unbroken series of successful gestures" (4) on the leisure-class stage. Nick's patronizing interest in the "poor young clerks who loitered in front of windows waiting until it was time for a solitary restaurant dinner" (44) seems not so much the futile identifying isolation of Eliot's Prufrock as it is the remembered empathy of one who is no longer there.

That "haunting loneliness," and his own fantasy "that I, too, was hurrying toward gayety and sharing their intimate excitement" remove him from the "poor young clerks" and incline him again toward Jordan. Just as the man who first asked him directions in West Egg "conferred on me the freedom of the neighborhood" (5), Jordan Baker confers on him a participant's ticket of admission to another world from which he had been excluded: "At first I was flattered to go places with her, because she was a golf champion, and everyone knew her name. Then it was something more. I wasn't actually in love, but I felt a sort of tender curiosity" (44).

Toward Jordan at this point Nick feels not love but a "sort of tender curiosity." Again he is the observer who would penetrate beneath affectations. Jordan's particular affectation is an aloofness, a detachment, an insolence that masks her competitive drive to excel, to be first. Her identity is as bound up with dominion as with being above ordinary pressures and desires, at least above caring about them. Nick, though, responds in Jordan's mode, from her rather superior point of view: "It made no difference to me. Dishonesty in a woman is a thing you never blame deeply—I was casually sorry, and then I forgot" (45).

In fact, the conversation they have with driving as the metaphor for human conduct shows that Nick really is as attracted to Jordan's carelessness as she is to his caution. He is indeed susceptible to upper-class flattery. Recall the moment when he brings to consciousness the likelihood that he loves Jordan. His revelation follows her calculated, casual remark: " 'I hate careless people. That's why I like you' " (45). Although he brakes the affair with his sense of the decency owed the home-town girl he is escaping, his admiration for the poster girl in Jordan comes out in his revulsion from the "faint mustache of perspiration" ungracing the old flame's upper lip after tennis. Jordan, we presume, is above such bodily commonness.

Nick's self-elevation to cardinal virtue, "I am one of the few honest people that I have ever met" (46), should be changed to read: clean, ordered, neat, and tidy within the context of stratified social position. As moral claim, his assertion is false. He'll be straight with Jordan and the nice girl from Minnesota, but, with the working girl, he'll "let it all blow quietly away." Sexuality within contexts of property and class is for Carraway necessarily more meaningful and more dutiful than it is beyond such considerations. What Nick views as moral is from critical perspective social, that is, pertaining to family and class.

Later, after Jordan has told him her version of Gatsby's past love and present dream of Daisy, Nick puts Jordan's attractiveness in terms of being and personality: "Suddenly I wasn't thinking of Daisy and Gatsby any more, but of this clean, hard, limited person, who dealt in universal skepticism, and who leaned back jauntily just within the circle of my arm. . . . Unlike Gatsby and Tom Buchanan, I had no girl whose disembodied face floated along the dark cornices and blinding signs, and so I drew up the girl beside me, tightening my arms. Her wan, scornful mouth smiled, and so I drew her up again closer, this time to my mouth" (61). In her tangibility she makes no demands upon Nick's imagination. Unlike Daisy Fay, she has no moments, no matter how isolated and fragmentary, of perception, grief, or sympathy.[2] She is only existent without complexity or qualification. Almost measurably, Carraway knows where he and she stand; he knows too that, unlike Daisy, she will never for any reason wander off the estate of her class and milieu.

For Nick, in business as in love, manners masquerade as morality. He handles economic propositions no differently than he does Jordan and her human limitations. When he consents to play Pandarus for Daisy and Gatsby, Gatsby offers him masked compensation: " 'It wouldn't take up much of your time and you might pick up a nice bit of money. It happens to be a rather confidential sort of thing' " (63).

As with Jordan's dishonesty, form, split off from substance, decides. Not because of criminality, possibly like the World Series fix, "but because the offer was obviously and tactlessly for a service rendered, I had no choice except to cut him off there" (63). Technically, one can say that such testimony witnesses Nick's honesty, but essentially he is more committed to the good form of middle-class manners and to his own self-making than he is to moral conduct. To accept a handout is both bad form and bad manners. One thinks Nick requires the illusion, at least, that his abilities are involved and needed, that he would be earning the money.

Gentility, snobbery, hypocrisy, manners as self-enhancement,

---

[2] I refer to Daisy's few, isolated moments of perception and loyalty to Gatsby, such as her tears for his "beautiful shirts," i.e., for him (70); and her indiscreet, indirect communication of love for Gatsby at the lunch preceding the catastrophe (90).

self-protection, self-concealment, above all a sensibility that re-
serves not judgments but feelings—before the catastrophe such
are the antennae Nick Carraway extends to that new world in
the East, to "the old island here that flowered once for Dutch
sailors' eyes" (137).

4

If that "old island" has been absorbed into a larger
continental destiny by history, then in the same way the holocaust of *The Great Gatsby* must strip all pretense of innocence
from Carraway and implicate him in the historical process, the
general human condition. With Nick, Fitzgerald calls up in a
highly particularized context the journey from innocence to experience, from ignorance to education and, perhaps, knowledge.
Since this pattern's given is that the young explorer will not
learn fully until experience has forced him to, the criteria for
judging Carraway are his actions after Gatsby's rejection and
murder. What must be examined are Nick's response to Gatsby's
death itself and those new choices he makes in his own life because of Gatsby's life and death.

What Nick feels after Gatsby is gone seems a terrific loneliness and a related loyalty. Vainly he tries to round up friends
and acquaintances who are human beings to witness the funeral.
But in the absence of notoriety and newspaper coverage, the
pendulum, as it had in Gatsby's life whenever the carnival was
broken off, swings over to isolation. Nick is predictably unsuccessful and, except for Owl-Eyes and Gatsby's father, to whom mansion and furniture are more real than his son had ever been, Nick
is the only mourner. If Owl-Eyes pronounces the gut benediction ("the poor son-of-a-bitch"), it is nevertheless left to Nick
to show in the context of his life the meaning of Gatsby's dream
and tragedy as a particular as well as a universal event in American history and culture. This Fitzgerald has Carraway do in a
threefold way. First, there unfolds, through memory, his recon-

nection to the Middle West of adolescence, then his Middle Westerner's contrast between East and West—artificial versus natural, nightmare versus reverie. In the second place Carraway resolves his eastern experience by encounters, one arranged with Jordan Baker, the other with Tom Buchanan, accidental. Finally, we must consider his reflections on Gatsby's dream and his actual nightmarish confrontation with a "new world material without being real" (123): the illustration from which Carraway generalizes about the universality of the American context.

Nick prepares us for his withdrawal into himself and abdication of historical engagement when he admits at Gatsby's funeral: "I tried to think about Gatsby for a moment, but he was already too far away" (133). (Memory of immediate horrors having failed him, Gatsby fast erased from consciousness, Carraway tries to grasp his own roots. Amnesia, for Carraway, is not general; memory becomes a tool of self-justification in experience, an ax with which to grind his ultimate American vision.)

Chartless in his surroundings, Carraway chooses to communicate his "vivid memory" of "coming back west from prep school and later college at Christmas time" (133). It seems that for the first time in the novel, consciousness mingles with nature in positive, dynamic polarity. What he excavates from his past is a memory of exhilaration which bears a similarity to the apprehension of America by the Dutch sailors. In his memory of the youthful return, that intense awareness of place identity begins as the train runs beyond Chicago into space—space which Nick soon elegizes as "that vast obscurity beyond the city, where the dark fields of the republic rolled on under the night" (137). One knows that sense of terrific space in the Middle West, as the land rushes into consciousness at night. No longer does one chart distance according to the dots of small towns; rather, the land is there, in new perspective, limitless and unknown, so that traveling through it one knows somewhat that fear and daring Columbus must have felt as he sailed across a world that geography said would end before his eyes. Certainly, on the prairies at night one has the sense of America yet to be civilized—yet, even, to be explored.

Immediately, however, Nick's language socializes his identity with the country. *His* Middle West consists of "the thrilling returning trains of my youth, and the street lamps and sleigh bells in the frosty dark and the shadows of holly wreaths thrown by lighted windows on the snow" (133–34). Security and safety, traditional family occasions: Nick conveys his insular sense of "growing up in the Carraway house in a city where dwellings are still called through decades by a family's name" (134). There appears an order about this middle-class, Middle-West society which composes Nick now. Still, Carraway sees clearly this world's limitations: "bored, sprawling, swollen towns beyond the Ohio, with their interminable inquisitions . . ." (134). No, what sends Nick home is his related vision of the East, no longer continent of dreams but rich ghetto of nightmare. "The East was haunted for me like that, distorted beyond my eyes' power of correction" (134); thus the theme of optometrist Eckleburg's sightless eyes reverberates to a new dissonance for the narrator who was once impersonal. Reality in the East has destroyed Carraway's capacity to see simultaneously within and without.

In any case the nightmare's imagery suggests contraries to Carraway's adolescent memory of the Middle West. Here no clear air or bracing snow, rather a "sullen, overhanging sky and a lustreless moon" (134); nature, too, is static and dead. Jewels and formal clothes create a contrived, artificial setting, almost a set from Nick's nightmare. Finally, contrary to the middle-western houses which contain in themselves identity, personality, and continuity, the stretcher-bearers cannot find the right house for the drunken woman. Clearly, there exists no right house. Her name too is unknown, nonexistent; like all other objects on this grotesque set, she is "material without being real," uninvested with sensibility, moral consciousness, or, indeed, any powers of consciousness. This eastern world horrifies Carraway because its very material, one-dimensional reality expresses its essential nothingness.

Seasonal allusions reinforce both the escapism of Carraway's return West as well as the necessity, given what he is, of the round trip. In winter, which is approaching, he will hibernate in the ancestral cave. Whereas Nick set out in late spring with "that *familiar* conviction that life was beginning over again with the summer" (5)—contrapuntally, his own metaphor comparing organic growth with how "things grow in fast movies" (5) grows out of an inorganic mode of perceptual and aesthetic fantasy; the summer has come with immobilizing heat and has finally borne a harvest of death. So that Carraway's last vision invokes a time-space pattern of history cyclical and static, a repetition forever of the attempt to make word flesh. Yet, as Gatsby failed to realize, that metamorphosis does not depend simply upon an "extraordinary gift for hope," "romantic readiness," or even "responsiveness" (4) generally. Perhaps the metamorphosis dooms itself as soon as it builds a mythic-religious framework as a set suitable for the stage of history. Certainly, in this particular theater—the white, post-Renaissance, Calvinist, mercantile-historical epoch—moral relationships depend upon sensibility and intelligence; above all they depend upon factual and conceptual understanding of the past. Good intentions are not enough; honesty is crucial. The laundry is too dirty.

Before he unloads his narrator's vision of universal defeat on our shoulders, Fitzgerald tries out Carraway's new sense of himself in his last relations with those he is leaving behind: Jordan Baker and Tom Buchanan. The meeting with Jordan seems disarming enough. She replays their conversation about carelessness and caution. This time, however, she accuses him, though still through the driving metaphor: " 'Well, I met another bad driver, didn't I? I mean it was careless of me to make such a wrong guess. I thought you were rather an honest, straightforward person. I thought it was your secret pride' " (135). For the first time Carraway's response is honest, though indirect: " 'I'm thirty,' I said. 'I'm five years too old to lie to myself and call it honor' " (135). The exchange exposes the sexual dimensions of the affair. Presumably, what Jordan labels "careless" in Nick is his refusal (a gut response to the holocaust) at least to pretend he loves her enough to marry her, a response she has a certain right to expect given his claims to honesty and morality. For in a relationship such as theirs the code provides marriage as the finale for sleeping together.

Nick's follow-up, again for the first and last time with a woman, expresses a certain closeness, an attachment, a hint of passion: "Angry, and half in love with her, and tremendously sorry, I turned away" (135). Perhaps, also for the first time, ambivalence flows genuinely and spontaneously from the experience. For once, Carraway does not use ambivalence to impose petty judgments on the world. Here I do not think he tries, as had been the case with earlier relationships, to evade the bonds of contact. Rather, at this point, he can no longer view Jordan's dishonesty and amorality as minor, even fetching flaws in a formally seductive portrait of a lady. Better isolation than either acceptance of selfish corruption or the pretense that these things do not exist in an essential way. Here, at last, moral reality outweighs for Carraway considerations of honor, manners, or what they in society call good form. Indeed, one feels that it is Jordan's coy reliance upon these pasteboard masks which turns Nick instinctively and silently away from her, body and consciousness united in action—small action, but action still.

With no transition, we witness the next scene in Carraway's drama of separation from the East. With Buchanan, his first response is the bodily impulse not to shake hands. Soon, however, Buchanan's aggression wins Nick to audience. In order to survive himself and to protect Daisy, he has turned over Gatsby's name and address to Wilson. But Buchanan clings to the false belief that Gatsby, not Daisy, ran down Myrtle Wilson. Now, at the moment (we hope) of truth, knowledge functions paralytically: "There was nothing I could say, except the one unutterable fact that it wasn't true" (136). Why UNUTTERABLE? Here and elsewhere, particularly in his universalizing reflections, Carraway projects a desire to be the only one who knows and broods about the truth. To recognize the taint in an evil world seems for him a means almost toward elite status. Even if we doubt his courage to face brutal Tom Buchanan, we must recognize, I think, the moral and epistemological superiority complex which leads Nick to dismiss Buchanan as a child unworthy even of hearing about sin, corruption, and viciousness. Nick only, it seems, has reached the use of reason. To depart from this sterilized eastern garden marks one as innocent; this innocence, Carraway seems to feel, is conferred upon one through grace after mere confession of complicity in the fallen world of human experience.

Carraway's inclination toward one version of reality—recall his precept: "life is much more successfully looked at from a single window, after all" (5)—shows itself further in his possessive attitude toward memories of Gatsby's life. He avoids a local taxi driver for fear this man too would have a story "all his own" about Gatsby and the accident. Finally, as prelude to his original-sin explanation of history and experience, he becomes again caretaker of manners and morals as he erases an obscene word from Gatsby's "white steps" (137). (Appearances, it now seems, are all that will keep the wolf of insanity from Carraway's own doorstep. Change the way the world looks, then stitch together an ordered vision from whole cloth.)

5

About Carraway's judgments on history and the nature of man two related questions stare us down. First, are the views and vision Nick Carraway's and not necessarily Fitzgerald's or our own? Second, how and to what extent are Carraway's analyses, judgments, and predictions contingent on his own background—his particular, psychological, social, economic, and cultural context, that total configuration of his history and personality?

> We have lingered in the chambers of the sea
> By sea-girls wreathed with seaweed red and brown
> Till human voices wake *us*, and *we* drown.[3]

So *we* beat on, boats against the current, borne back cease· lessly into the past (137, my italics).

Now I invoke the same principles of distance and detachment between Carraway and Fitzgerald that critics generally are willing to respect with Prufrock and T. S. Eliot. Critical with these two narrators, and with almost every narrator, is the distinction between witness and judge. Both Prufrock and Carraway are valid witnesses: Prufrock to his own hollow psychological condition; Carraway to particular facts and circumstances, events in his own and Gatsby's history. But as Prufrock has no basis other than insecurity for including us (that unspecified yet all-inclusive "we") in his vision of sexual fantasy and fear of real bodies and persons, neither can Carraway legitimately judge all Americans only on the evidence of what he has witnessed and experienced with himself and Gatsby. Such doom is a subtle form of hubris; i.e., since I am responding thus and so to my situation (particulars conveniently disappear), therefore, so will all of you respond. Both narrators forget that personality, history, and reality are, in Iris Murdoch's words, "contingent, messy, boundless, infinitely particular and endlessly still to be explained." [4]

What Carraway does is to put a historical event in a metaphysical category. The polarity swings from man's imagination, his "capacity for wonder," to the material of the universe, "a fresh green breast of the new world" (137). The word "pan-

---

[3] T. S. Eliot, "The Love Song of J. Alfred Prufock," *The Complete Poems and Plays: 1909–1950* (New York: Harcourt, Brace and World, 1952), p. 7. My italics.

[4] Iris Murdoch, "The Sublime and the Beautiful Revisited," *The Yale Review*, vol. 49, p. 260.

dered," chosen to describe the qualitative relationship between man and matter, reveals Carraway's dualist, original-sin bias. The rhetoric itself gives him away. First, he alludes to the Dutch sailors, particular men who came to America in a particular cultural and historical context. Perhaps because of the colonial-mercantile nature of their journey, he shifts his paradigm to universal man, man enchanted outside time: "Its vanished trees, the trees that had made way for Gatsby's house, had once pandered in whispers to the last and greatest of all human dreams; for a transitory enchanted moment man must have held his breath in the presence of this continent, compelled into an aesthetic contemplation he neither understood nor desired, face to face for the last time in history with something commensurate to his capacity for wonder" (137).

Note the dichotomies between nature and history, beauty and labor, imagination and rationality. Implicit is the metaphysic that natural objects and the physical universe rarely provide realities worthy of human imagination. Yet Carraway puts the responsibility for despoiling America upon the perception and appetite of man: "aesthetic contemplation he neither understood nor desired." So the unknown beauty of pre-European America both "pandered in whispers" (beckoned seductively) to man (Dutch sailors, possibly disassociated from Dutch merchants and owners) and compelled him into "aesthetic contemplation." Not consciousness but "aesthetic contemplation." Maybe what "pandered" means historically is that the undefiled, unowned (America before property in a capitalist sense would have had a special appeal to landless Europeans) continent seemed to encourage "the last and greatest of all human dreams." Now I think Carraway uses "pandered" to suggest that by its overwhelming and original beauty America for a moment legitimized an essentially fraudulent (for him) dream. That dream I take to be the embodiment, simultaneously in and out of time and space, as we think of those concepts historically, changingly, the embodiment of man's "unutterable visions,"

the aesthetic union of mind with all its Cartesian baggage
of self-created, self-dependent systems and that which is perishable, subject to change, finally beyond the mind's control
in the universe. Here history refers to a series of encounters during which man, in those rare moments when his imagination discovers a suitable object, himself lacks the sensibility necessary to
"aesthetic contemplation." For this reason—not, in fact, man's
disability but his failure—Carraway binds "aesthetic contemplation" to the timeless but fragile "transitory, enchanted moment"
and opposes aesthetic reality to history, a succession of particular
actions, events, and circumstances at distinct times and in distinct places.

The question has become: why this incompatibility between
history and aesthetic sensibility? Why has man worn out the
world? Previously, one has sensed the taint which for Carraway
clings to matter. It is the incarnation myth and metaphor: the
word or spirit *descends* to flesh or body. Earlier Carraway para-
digmed Gatsby's choice of Daisy as a marriage between "unutterable visions" and "perishable breath." Involved in that union
is recognition of otherness, mortality, and history insofar as history conveys the stage on which individual men have brief lives
and then depart forever. For no matter how far imagination's
visions may seem to reach beyond physical territory, finally they
must be acted out within bodies whose terrains are both limited
and final. Gatsby, in the beginning, unconsciously feels these
necessities, but after the experience, ironically, after the pressures
of history, Daisy becomes for him more an "unutterable vision"
than a woman in a given context of a particular time and place,
not to mention a particular history. So, contrary to Carraway's
platonic rhetoric and metaphor, the real deceiver is male imagination insofar as it lulls man from awareness of the hardships
which will confront him in the very otherness, the unknown of
nature. Man then projects ideal perfection upon nature and
other persons to conceal the possessive desires of his own dark
heart.

When Carraway comes particularly to Gatsby, one feels him slip into allusions to Eden, primal myth of Western culture whose article of faith, at best, is that nature followed man into *essential* imperfection, corruption, and evil; and, at worst, that evil found its original, tangible presence in a temptation offered to man by nature or at least in nature's guise. In any case Carraway begs the question of historical analysis and explanation. He talks of "the old unknown world" (again, why UNKNOWN?), then connects Gatsby to that first, mere projected moment of "aesthetic contemplation": "He had come a long way to this blue lawn, and his dream must have seemed so close that he could hardly fail to grasp it. He did not know that it was already behind him, somewhere back in that vast obscurity beyond the city, where the dark fields of the republic rolled on under the night" (137). Difficult to translate the metaphorical journey into history. Easy, however, to identify it with the Calvinist world view. Naive with his dream of election, Gatsby did not know that in America the issue had already closed in damnation. One must, I think, go from a Calvinist account of the Fall and its consequences to an analogously determinist version of history. Here the republic equals historical innocence and possibility—its place, nature beyond the urban pale, almost a pastoral myth. Empire yields to decadence and corruption: hopes washed out, possibility vanished, as with Rome its place the city, man's replacement of the natural world.

One senses in Carraway's evocation of the changing continent a loss of intensity between place and consciousness. "Vast obscurity," "dark fields" summon an America unknown, unincorporated into any rational property system. But as there comes with ownership a certain death to the object, a dissolution, in the owner's view, of its independence and integrity, so the property system brought to the continent and its exploiters an end to aesthetic impulse. For property often makes the object an appendage of ego.

Not only did beauty become less real, less critical than wealth until wealth became beauty, but, worst of all, relation, in America, between property structure and the land went forth on an increasingly abstract level. Men rushed across the breadth of this continent plundering and acquiring, not discovering, certainly not contemplating. The Indians whose "identity with this country" was as tangible as its geography were largely annihilated, always subjugated, dealt with as objects as they are dealt with to this moment. Men did not want to settle and live as human beings in relationship to a unique and particular place; their strongest impulse was to race to the last frontier of America. As if migration could somehow remove the blood from their hands, the horror from their souls. Unwilling to give justice and real citizenship to black and Indian Americans their descendants award democracy to Vietnamese and Thais. "I cannot bear the truth" has become an American anthem. Its corollary in action: "Love me or I'll kill you."

Historically, Carraway's pastoral, Edenic allusions go back to the birth of this nation as republic, when it, in Jefferson's words, branded "as cowardly the idea that the human mind is incapable of further advances." [5] Now Carraway forgets or does not regard as central the fact that this republic owed its life as much to its institution of slavery and its colonial policy (really, a policy of extermination) toward the Indians as it did to the courage and democratic institutions of its citizens. The analogy implied with Rome also recalls the transition from republic to an empire largely incapable of re-examining historical process in relation to those past and present assumptions which determine the nation's course.

In any case one must guess at Carraway's version of American history from Revolution until Civil War. But the latter event and the ensuing opportunity for second birth or "Reconstruction" is, in fact and as allusively presented in Gatsby, a turning

[5] Thomas Jefferson as quoted by Marius Bewley in The Eccentric Design: Form in the Classic American Novel (New York: Columbia University Press, 1959), p. 265.

point in our history. Three threads are woven into a plainly marked texture: that of Carraway's great-uncle, that of miner Cody exploring on behalf of the "material interests," that of the Southern resonance infiltrating the novel through Buchanan. First of all, Carraway has presented the Civil War as the historical event from which an ancestor gave his family economic ballast in Minneapolis-St. Paul. Great-uncle Carraway saw in the war a mercantile opportunity. Armies need hardware. Invest some money—three hundred dollars, I believe—in a substitute, and one will reap profits a thousandfold. So also do growing industrial nations need hardware. Dan Cody, archetypal settler-plunderer of the West, required hardware, if not for his own hands, then to sell to those who worked the mines whose rights he owned. As this novel summarizes the late nineteenth century, that period which many hoped would reverse the trend of property and empire, would humanize America, that age merely confirms and perfects the process of accumulation. Instead of knowing some of America dynamically, immediately, aesthetically, the urge was to own it all, aggressively, mechanically, abstractly.

To be fair, that early Carraway did stake out a small claim and sink roots. This is why third-generation Minnesotan Nick can return "unutterably aware"—intense experience always denies him articulation and communication—of his "identity with this country." Yet roots and continuity, individual and historical, are missing in all others who live in this novel's world. Henry C. Gatz, insistent as he is about his own name, worships Gatsby's house, unaware of its absurd nonrelation to the land on which it stands. Dan Cody, who owns great stretches of America, lives nowhere but on a yacht itself rarely at anchor. He seeks aboard the Tuolomee (named for a river in the Alaskan gold fields) further buried treasure in the West Indies and the Barbary Coast. No Columbus, this "civilized" pirate's contribution to culture is to discontent easterners with their lives: as an escape he offers them models of mining-town saloons, rodeos, and the violent, usually fruitless expeditions toward unverified rivers of gold.

But the most solid, most damning representative of postbellum America has to be Tom Buchanan, whose racism and manner of the plantation owner revolts even Daisy and Jordan, whose "white girlhoods" were passed in Louisville. One recalls that his presidential namesake, James Buchanan, owed his 1856 election to fourteen slave states, only five free, and that in his inaugural he called for an end to agitation against slavery and supported the policy of noninterference with slavery in the states and "popular sovereignty" in the territories. Indeed, Tom Buchanan's opinions and life-style conjure up the new Southern aristocracy who grew even richer because of alliances with Northern industrial capital and technology. Strangely, Carraway is totally inexplicit about the sources of Buchanan's wealth, yet we know that he's inherited it and that its well will not dry up.

Given Buchanan's presence as the novel's power, physically and economically, his behavior and attitudes become important, if no less preposterous. His is the sexual schizophrenia associated with the white owner in the American South. His relations with women, as well as with all other persons and things, are hierarchical, based impeccably upon training and self-interest. To satisfy the demands of his body, he keeps Myrtle Wilson—keeps her, that is, compartmentalized in a lower middle-class world. Like spoil, she is replaceable. Daisy, being his property, he owns. In a sense, Daisy is a grail to Tom, too. When Myrtle shouts his wife's name, Tom breaks her nose. Daisy is the America he conserves. It is Buchanan's view of love that while the man roams, the woman stays at home, faithful and loving because she knows (or else should know) that " 'I always come back, and in my heart I love her all the time' " (100). (In the showdown, Daisy yields to Tom, not for love, but because he, not Jay Gatsby, is proprietor over stability and wealth. Her composite being includes money, class, leisure time, and tastes; the place of her

being is "wherever people played polo and were rich together"—
the world as Buchanan's estate. Money yes, but old money, solid
money, money backed up by the continent itself.)

What lingers more depressingly even than these contexts are
Carraway's last words on Gatsby. How can he say: "Gatsby
turned out all right at the end"? How can he blame merely
"what foul dust floated in the wake of his dreams" (4)? He can
do so only because such a view of innocence frees an individual
from responsibility for historical, cultural, and moral contexts,
frees him from responsibility to anything but his own dreams
and fantasies. Nick, one suspects out of self-justification, cannot
bear the assignment of essential relationship between himself
and his context. So Gatsby must remain free from involvement
in the disintegration and corruption of America, despite his complicity with bootlegging, blackmail, and the Black Sox scandal.
If we grant this abstraction of the individual from culture, then
surely Nick, who is so strict a judge, so pessimistic a historian,
will be held responsible only for his own salvation.

Finally, Nick Carraway, individual, is not our concern. Our
focus must be historical; therefore, platonic-Calvinist readings of
the American past are not relevant except as backdrops to the
process of events in and beyond the novel. The cyclical, mythic
mode may have been *the* way; for us it is *one* way, an explanation which introduces and conceals elements in history more rationalist and differentiated. So we have got to be clear about
Gatsby's contexts, about his single-mindedness. Is his dream itself a nightmare? Once that dream is, in fact, gone, does reaching for it automatically turn destructive? If so, isn't it almost
literally insane to lament it as Carraway does? Don't we have to
judge this novel, its victim and its narrator, in relation to the
greater culture alluded to throughout?

6

"In dreams begins responsibility" Yeats recalled at the beginning of one of his volumes, and that is the assertion we must make about Gatsby and the American dream generally. What Gatsby overlooks are the connections between culture and personality. He pursues Daisy without relation to objects, except (an overwhelming exception) as their accumulation is necessary to attain her. He nourishes the fantasy that if one keeps his goal a pure dream, keeps the focus fixed on the same being, nothing else that exists is real or necessary. The logic turns vicious, though, for Gatsby comes more and more to define himself, as best he can—and his best is shoddy and affected—in terms of Daisy's world. Thus when he finally has Daisy again, he desperately and insecurely diverts her from himself to his possessions.

> Look how the sunset catches my house.
> See its period bedrooms.
> Feel all my English shirts.
> Listen to my man, Klipspringer, play my grand piano
> In my Marie Antoinette music room.

He has, during and because of his five-year quest, lost the very contingent "responsiveness" which, one imagines, moved Daisy to him in the first place.

Gatsby's house indeed might as well be a houseboat sailing up and down the Long Island coast, as the rumors contend. "Material without being real," it is both as intangible and as monstrously tangible as his dream. To Gatsby himself it is never real, unless for the moment he wondrously discovers it while showing it to Daisy, who at once sees the house as grotesque and dislocated from its time and place. The house itself? "A factual imitation of some Hôtel de Ville in Normandy" (6). Its brief cycle of ownership has descended from German brewer to dreaming bootlegger. Soon Daisy will find Gatsby himself as irrelevant to her world and culture, to herself, as is his house. So also Gatsby's nightmare began when he wedded his "unutterable visions" to her "perishable breath." We're talking about a particular cultural vision. Even before he met Daisy, Gatsby's focus was upon that "vast, vulgar, and meretricious beauty" of the America over which goddess Daisy presided. Or, to paraphrase a question Nicole Warren will ask late in *Tender Is The Night*: How long can the person, the woman in a Daisy Fay transcend the universals of her culture? In America, clearly, not very long. An interlude at best. Like the song said:

> "In the meantime,
> In between time—" (72)

Jay Gatsby was doomed from the start by "just the sort of Jay Gatsby that a seventeen-year-old boy" *in early twentieth-century small-town America* "would be likely to invent" (75). Archetypically American are the materials of his self-creation. True last will and testament seems the biographical document Henry C. Gatz carries East to his son's funeral. On the inside cover of a Hopalong Cassidy comic book read SCHEDULE and as afterthought and afterword: GENERAL RESOLVES. In stark relief issues Gatsby's cultural context before he leaves home for St. Olaf's and thereafter for Dan Cody's service. The SCHEDULE maps out a regimen for every hour of the day. In addition to the Victorian notion of a sane mind in a sound body, there is the implicit encouragement toward ambition, toward the proverbial tradition of American greatness. Worst of all is the proverbial mode which dissociates success from the uses of power.

But young Gatz looked beyond Poor Richard to the master himself in his adolescent determination to "study needed inventions" (131). Yes, between 7:00 and 9.00 P.M. after his self-instruction in "elocution and poise." The GENERAL RESOLVES catalogue those practical-moralistic doses of cultural codliver oil at the root of Franklin's reading of experience (his public reading, that is):

No wasting time at Shafers or (a name, indecipherable)
No more smokeing or chewing
Bath every other day
Read one improving book or magazine per week
Save $5.00 (crossed out) $3.00 per week
Be better to parents (132)

Yet annihilating it all to the sixteen-year-old's imagination is
the paper it is written on. No *tabula rasa* this Hopalong Cassidy
comic book. Hopalong's white horse and chivalric cowboy adventures utter the fantasy far more graphically and kinetically
than do the prosaic Alger-Franklin schedules and resolves. Why
shouldn't the young provincial just go and *be* a hero in an America beyond the small town? Hopalong Cassidy has no family
either, no continuous identity beyond hat and horse, no responsibilities other than to preserve law and order and keep crime
rates low in the Wild West. Who can doubt the inevitability
of James Gatz's flight from North Dakota or his creation of Jay
Gatsby? Or his switch of filial allegiance from shabby, powerless
Henry C. Gatz, like St. Joseph merely a serf in the vineyards, to
Dan Cody, patriarch of expansion, man of action and entrepreneur both, a man who could beat the Robber Barons at their
game of violent ownership, then draw their jealous admiration
at his physical exploits in a Wild West Show? Quite clearly,
Fitzgerald means Dan Cody to be a true and historical version
of Hopalong Cassidy.

7

So in each echelon of the world Nick Carraway enters
we find options closed out; in himself because of the failure of
sensibility and moral imagination, with the Buchanans because
of a lack of "fundamental decencies." In the case of Gatsby the
end precedes the beginning because that man fails to plant his
identity in subsoil, in earth more responsive to the aesthetic impulse than the twin shoals of an ahistorical yet all too historic

false heroic (Alger-Cassidy) *and* a complementary ethic of salvation by accumulation (Franklin-Cody). But what of Carraway himself? He is guilty neither of the amoral cruelty of the Buchanan set—like him or not, he does possess some capacity for relationship—nor of Gatsby's delusion that man can simultaneously ignore and conquer history through a platonic self-creation derived from and modeled on that very same history and culture. What are we, the *we* whom Carraway invokes in his last prophetic sentence, to do with his absolute judgment that aesthetic sensibility has, does, will fail to penetrate history and culture in America? The assumption is so total and so based on a fable whose contexts are so relatively few, it seems we've got to dissociate Fitzgerald from Carraway's vision or, if that distorts the structure and spirit of the novel, then assault Fitzgerald himself with our objections. Somewhere, so goes the latter view, the novelist's own critical judgment and negative capability failed him. Wittingly or unwittingly, Fitzgerald has become the property of his own narrator. This reading has had sufficient exposition.[6] It is, I think, false.

I oppose that interpretation, first, on formal grounds, because of what I believe to be the novel's contingent, contextual principle, and, second, on those biographical grounds most often used contrarily to join Fitzgerald to Carraway in a perceptually Siamese way. It seems to me that, *given the nature and goal of his own quest*, Carraway's conclusions are formally and morally as reasonable as the world he encounters. Even a narrator, after all, can expect to receive no better objects and goals than those he seeks. And Nick Carraway comes East for no other reason than to make his fortune, and thereby himself. True, the stolidity of the Middle West bores him to restlessness. He would have the

---

6 Several critics, among them Leslie Fiedler in *An End to Innocence* (Boston: Beacon Press, 1955), and recently, Richard Lehan (see n. 9 below), charge Fitzgerald with a failure of critical intelligence in that, they feel, he has not put sufficient distance between his characters'—especially Carraway and Diver's— failures and his own.

excitement of a world less charted, more charged. But the meta-phor for his identity is economic; he moves from hardware (solid, permanent commodity) to bonds (paper projections of values at a given time contingent upon a certain set of circumstances). Since Carraway would define and establish himself in a mercan-tile profession (a bond salesman is almost a money-seller, cer-tainly a money-changer), how can he expect the world he dis-covers to be anything other than a society of accumulation, a world whose only exception, Gatsby, has for his dream object a golden girl, a King Midas's daughter, and who can achieve the dream only if he masters the culture of money? We, therefore, have got to stand back from the frame of Carraway's narrative portrait, to see his judgment and prediction as true, inevitable, or universal *only* given the cultural context he and those in his fable have chosen for their world.

Fitzgerald, I believe, would teach the following lesson: under-stand and then beware of this context. I say *this* context, be-cause its pervasiveness, its terrific powers of seduction are driven home by its being the only real context. For in *The Great Gatsby* "money is the root of all evil" is refined to read: money is the root of all culture, and, for Carraway, possibly the root of all nature as well. In addition to contextual structure, Fitzgerald relies, as does T. S. Eliot in the case of Prufrock, on seductive, romantic, and, at the same time, paralytic language to sepa-rate us from the narrator. Recall Prufrock's fantasy of sea-girls ". . . riding seaward on the waves / Combing the white hair of the waves blown back." [7] Here we have elegiacally the dead sea of Prufrock's unconscious, where his prurience does not have to grant the complexity or even the existence of other beings, what Yeats faced as "the mire and the fury of human veins." Just so, as an excuse for not facing history, which involves all human desire, Carraway offers "that vast obscurity beyond the city" and that futile beating of wings that afflicts, in Carraway's judgment,

[7] Eliot, "The Love Song of J. Alfred Prufrock," *Complete Poems,* p. 7.

anyone who swims forward against history's current. What better defense of one's own paralysis than the prophecy that all has
been decided, that history itself is lost?

There is a tension between language and form which an artist
has got to resolve if he is to reveal his vision and sensibility; for
however complex these may be, they will show in art a coherence and a clarity. We have seen how on one occasion Daisy's
spontaneous language of music creates an aesthetic presence
"bringing out a meaning in each word that it had never had
before and would never have again" (82). Or recall Carraway's
comment after Gatsby listens to Daisy "with a rush of emotion"
at their reunion: "I think that voice held him most, with its
fluctuating, feverish warmth, because it couldn't be overdreamed
—that voice was a deathless song" (73). Deathless like the song
of Keats's nightingale; deathless in relation to the ongoing motion of life. No categorical description such as Gatsby's " 'Her
voice is full of money' " (91), even when legitimately confirmed
by Carraway in properly economic metaphors, can dispel this or
any aesthetic phenomenon's own integrity and possibility. I
mention these examples of music because in his soliloquy Carraway abandons that dynamic tension between language and form
when he has richly romantic tonalities serve a vision that has
immobilized history and personality. He, it seems to me, is
finally an aesthetic pander, who, like a witch with a lullaby,
croons others to death, not sleep, because of his own sickness.

Biographical data, in my judgment, increase rather than di-
minish the distance between Fitzgerald and Carraway. It was,
after all, as Fitzgerald wrote to John O'Hara in 1933, his own
position as outsider which forced him as man and novelist to
understand difference and particularity among socio-economic
contexts:

> I am half black Irish and half old American stock with the
> usual exaggerated ancestral pretensions. The black Irish half
> of the family had the money and looked down upon the Mary-
> land side of the family who had, and really had, that certain

series of reticences and obligations that go under the poor old shattered word "breeding." (modern form "inhibitions"). . . . So if I were elected King of Scotland tomorrow after graduating from Eton, Magdalene to Guards, with an embryonic history which tied me to the Plantagenets, I would still be a parvenu. . . . I would be capable of going to Podunk on a visit and being absolutely booed and overawed by its social system, not from timidity but simply because of an inner necessity of starting my life and my self-justification over again at scratch in whatever new environment I may be thrown.[8]

Now one has got to decide whether when he gave Carraway a Scotch-Presbyterian background instead of Irish-Catholic ancestry like his own, Fitzgerald was creating a *different* person whom he could view with powers of separation, or whether, as Richard Lehan argues, he was creating a projection of his own real and imagined safe and sane failure with whom he enjoyed thorough identification. Lehan is very literal about his parallels:

The return to the West is really a form of escape, a matter of Fitzgerald's own nostalgia about his boyhood. When Nick goes home, Fitzgerald is recalling his own sense of youth—the parties, the old friends, the trains happily crowded with handsome prep-school and college students returning for Christmas vacation, perhaps even Fitzgerald's own return home to finish his first novel after his failure in New York advertising—and he fails to consider the Midwest as a place of provincial conformity from which Nick had been trying to escape, along with the many characters in the novels of Sinclair Lewis, Sherwood Anderson, Glenway Wescott, and Floyd Dell.[9]

Even Nick sees the "Midwest as a place of provincial conformity," but goes home anyway because, in his view, no better alternatives exist. But the real question is about Fitzgerald's control over his material.

[8] Andrew Turnbull, ed., *The Letters of F. Scott Fitzgerald* (New York: Charles Scribner's Sons, 1963), p. 503.
[9] Richard Lehan, *F. Scott Fitzgerald and the Craft of Fiction* (Carbondale: Southern Illinois University Press, 1966), p. 174.

Certainly, to give Carraway a moderately successful Calvinist background steadies the scales midway between the book's dominant poles of election and damnation, dream and nightmare, myth and history. Not only is Carraway's background more typically American than Fitzgerald's; in addition, the father's stock of proverbial truth and material hardware gives him a certain authority upon which Nick can depend and from which he draws nourishment and identity in an America whose Cartesian imperative Nick has discovered to be "I own, therefore I am."

Fitzgerald, on the other hand, had, after success and marriage, no pull to retreat into adolescent background. Neither did he have a safe adolescent background into which he could retreat. His father, Edward Fitzgerald, built no wholesale hardware business, but went bankrupt in the 1880's behind a small wicker furniture business. For a while he worked as a salesman for Procter & Gamble in Buffalo, but he lost that job; so the family moved back to St. Paul, where Edward Fitzgerald became a *wholesale grocery salesman*—a job, Arthur Mizener guesses, "probably obtained through the old McQuillan connection." [10] Thus Fitzgerald's heritage gave him no crutches. He broke with Catholicism. He became a novelist, in sharp distinction both to his father's salesman positions and to his grandfather McQuillan's wholesale grocery business. In the thirties he joined the Communist party. In any case, Fitzgerald's journey, in times of disillusionment and despair, was always into himself. So that rather than changing details of his own past to disguise his essentially close identity with Carraway, it seems more likely that he selected with care social and historical details that placed Carraway in a context unmistakably distinct from his own.

Finally, reflect on a Fitzgerald memoir which, though written a dozen or more years after *Gatsby*, brings into wider biographical focus the relationship of Fitzgerald and his whole generation to the burdens of American empire:

[10] Arthur Mizener, *The Far Side of Paradise* (Boston: Houghton Mifflin, 1949), p. 16.

We were born to power and intense nationalism. We did not have to stand up in a movie house and recite a child's pledge to the flag to be aware of it. We were told, individually and as a unit, that we were a race that could potentially lick ten others of any genus. This is not a nostalgic article for it has a point to make—but we began life in post-Fauntleroy suits (often a sailor's uniform as a taunt to Spain). Jingo was the lingo—we saw plays named *Paul Revere* and *Secret Service* and raced toy boats called the *Columbia* and the *Reliance* after the cup defenders. We carved our own swords whistling, *Way Down in Colon Town*, where we would presently engage in battle with lesser breeds.[11]

So does Fitzgerald re-create his early milieu. So does he evoke critically an early twentieth-century culture of power which cut across class and other lines in America. But for him history was never without points of demarcation. "That America," he concludes, "passed away somewhere between 1910 and 1920." [12] Presumably, he is talking about his and his generation's abrupt consciousness, with World War I, of their nation's hypocrisy between rhetoric and policy, between democratic ideals and the ongoing facts of empire. Here, and I think in the pages of *Gatsby*, Fitzgerald notes the life cycle of American culture and the symptoms of its disease. But if it should die, he feels, as he said of Wordsworth, "no compulsion to pass away with it." If American culture, as he and we know it, should die of surfeit, that does not mean all culture must die. In *The Great Gatsby* Fitzgerald would have us regard Carraway's absolute finalities and closed prophecies with Yeats's "cold eye." At one and the same time he warns us against paralysis, and spells out, unflinchingly, the great odds in the way of moral, historical, and aesthetic reconstruction.

[11] Previously unpublished essay by Fitzgerald, "My Generation," *Esquire*, 7' (October, 1968), p. 121.
[12] *Ibid.*

three

Tender Is the Night: The two versions—a note on form

Fitzgerald's fullest reflection on the aesthetics of *Tender Is the Night* comes in a letter to John Peale Bishop, at the time of the novel's publication in April, 1934.

> You would be the first to feel that the intention in the two books was entirely different, that (to promote myself momentarily) *Gatsby* was shooting at something like *Henry Esmond* while this was shooting at something like *Vanity Fair*. The dramatic novel has canons quite different from the philosophical, now called psychological, novel. One is a kind of *tour de force* and the other a confession of faith. It would be like comparing a sonnet sequence with an epic.
>
> The point of my letter which survives is that there were moments all through the book where I could have pointed up dramatic scenes, and I *deliberately* refrained from doing so because the material itself was so harrowing and highly charged that I did not want to subject the reader to a series of nervous shocks in a novel that was inevitably close to whoever read it in my generation.
>
> Contrariwise, in dealing with figures as remote as are a bootlegger and crook to most of us, I was not afraid of heightening and melodramatizing any scenes; . . . I believe it was Ernest Hemingway who developed to me, in conversation, that the dying fall was preferable to the dramatic ending under certain con-

ditions, and I think we both got the germ of the idea from Conrad.[1]

Understatement then detaches an artist *from* whatever or whomever he might have essential identification *with;* whereas overstatement brings artist and audience closer *to* that *from* which they may be ordinarily remote. According to Fitzgerald's canon, the dramatic novel perceives and creates its world in dazzling, externally dynamic strokes, but the philosophical or psychological novel captures its readers by a different strategy. It evokes its world, often a world of impressionist patterns, and leaves that world to reverberate the total composition back and forth through the receiving consciousness. Although the two modes are neither incompatible nor mutually exclusive, reality in *Gatsby* comes across through statement, especially in its ending of overstatement and finality, while in *Tender Is the Night*, with its title and its ending of fading, dying impression, worlds come and go, appear and disappear. Except our own worlds into which, painfully, we are led once more.

Clearly, literary criticism of what Fitzgerald calls the "philosophical" or "psychological" novel requires canons other than those appropriate to the "dramatic" novel. Needed is reflective exegesis, a network of inner and outer connections. For not only is *Tender Is the Night* richer in focus, technique, texture, and sympathy than *The Great Gatsby*, but its roots go far deeper into American experience, not to mention the imperial system. The novel anatomizes the disintegrations and metamorphoses of personality and consciousness in a fragmenting Western world order from 1917 to 1930. Indeed, complexities of consciousness, history, and form in *Tender Is the Night* not only evoke, but sometimes create American culture.

As soon as he decides to read *Tender Is the Night*, a tough decision confronts any reader. Which version should he pick up?

---

[1] Andrew Turnbull, ed., *The Letters of F. Scott Fitzgerald* (New York: Charles Scribner's Sons, 1963), p. 363.

Where is the best point to begin reading? Best to define that choice.

Version 1: 1934, pp. 1–315

Book I: Chapter I begins with a moving picture of the Riviera and Rosemary's arrival there, goes chronologically to Nicole's collapse after Peterson's murder. June–July, 1925.

Book II: Chapter I jumps back to Dick Diver in Vienna in 1917; goes chronologically to his marriage and Nicole's summary of their life together until July, 1925. With Chapter XI, Book II leapfrogs Book I to August, 1925, then proceeds, again chronologically, to November, 1928, and Diver's catastrophe in Rome, Chapter XXIII.

Book III: From Diver's return to the clinic in Zurich to his departure from the Riviera, and finally, the Chapter XIII coda of Nicole Barban's double exposure snapshots of Diver as he wanders through upstate New York.

So the impressionist time shift places Chapters I through X of Book II after Book I's June through July action of 1925 instead of before it.

Version 2: rearranged early in 1939 by Fitzgerald and published by Scribner's Sons in 1953 as the second of that edition's *Three Novels*, pp. 1–334.

Book I: *Case History*, 1917–19. Goes from Chapter I, with Dick Diver in Vienna in the spring of 1917 to Chapter IX, June of 1919 when Dick and Nicole are thrown together, this time for good.

Book II: *Rosemary's Angle*, 1919–25. From a scene of marriage negotiations between Dick and Baby to Chapter XIII, a July afternoon during Rosemary's stay in Paris with the Divers.

Book III: *Casualties*, 1925 (July to August). From the battle-field tour to Rosemary's departure, the Divers' return to the Riviera.

Book IV: *Escape*, 1925–29. Goes from Christmas at Gstaad through Diver's catastrophe in Rome.

Book V: *The Way Home*, 1929–30. Dick's return to the clinic after his disastrous trip to America and Rome until the novel's end—chronological throughout.

The continued existence of each version together with the formation of almost warring factions of readers raises all those issues central to the nature and flexibility of the modern novel. Ultimately, form and its chosen vision of time decide such questions as the relationship between history and consciousness, object and mind, causality and chance. With *Tender Is the Night* the problem of form comes down to Fitzgerald's own doubts about the nature of time and personality. How does one know a person? What limitations are there in the very processes of seeing and knowing? Does fidelity to chronological or impressionist time schemes determine which notion of personality will motivate a novelist?

I'll begin with the obvious. There is the chronological assumption that there is a past and a present, that events often break down into beginning, middle, and end. And the impressionist notion that, no matter what the possible order of things, we know reality discontinuously in an associational mode—in short, that the world is arranged in no necessary order. Both visions have claims on legitimacy, and there should not be any final incompatibility. For each time-set is about something different; each develops its perceptions from a distinct and valid focus. Chronology yields a basic insight *about the facts and rhythms of existence*; i.e., birth, maturity, and death are accurate descriptions of a process which goes on not only in life but in history. Equally, the impressionist vision of time, not as sequential but as spatial, fragmented, disconnected, speaks of *how we know* consciousness and through modes of consciousness the world beyond it. In order to connect consciousness and history one must construct a floating bridge between these two modes of time and perception. To understand history, to both integrate and distinguish past from present, one must get close to individual consciousness. Whole layers of past experience may lay buried from memory until a chance association in the present sets consciousness into a wider motion. Even though there may be distinguishable realms of past and present, their true relationship, and, therefore, our history, may elude us unless sensitivity to tones, nuances, and rhythms of consciousness summon up those old, long-denied, longer-concealed facts. Such integration between chronology and psychic, spatial time, between history and consciousness, I seek to find in *Tender Is the Night* through the medium of personality, through the relationship of living beings to their anchors in the past.

Certainly, in *Tender Is the Night*, Version I, Fitzgerald plainly suggests by placing Diver's early life in the middle of the novel that one knows experience in no necessary order. To jumble chronology implies that chronological time is arbitrary and illusory artifice, that, in reality, no such consistent order governs Diver's life or lives generally. More positively, Fitzgerald's pattern of middle Diver, early Diver, later Diver asserts the fragmentary nature of man's perceptions, man's actions, and, finally, man's relationship to and power over circumstances. There is, in short, no one way to see, to act, to tell a story. Chronological order can deceive and mislead because it seems to commit perception to a natural, a necessary, a given structure of reality, if not to an inevitable causality. But also, in relation to human personality, chronology may posit being and identity as essential, that is, assume the existence of an indestructible core at the bottom of a personality. I refer to the conviction that a person may remain distinct from his context or set of circumstances, distinct from his world. Chronology may, therefore, in its will-

ingness to carry heroic baggage, encourage total belief in qualities of being that are stable, permanent, and self-determining.
Contrarily, in the first version of *Tender Is the Night*, Fitzgerald
follows the Ford-Conrad perception that in life one does not encounter persons and their reservoirs of experience in a chronological fashion. Instead, as with Diver, we begin at some contingent, associational point in an individual life, gradually learn
more, then at some point or moment discover in the past a true
beginning. Or, as Ford Madox Ford posited the relationship
between time and consciousness: "You meet an English gentleman at your golf club. He is beefy, full of health, the moral of
the boy from an English Public School of the finest type. You
discover gradually that he is hopelessly neurasthenic. . . . To
get such a man in fiction you could not begin at his beginning
and walk his life chronologically to the end. You must first get
him in with a strong impression, and then work backwards and
forwards over his past." [2] According to this psychic epistemol-
ogy, consciousness resembles a keyboard across which the scales
of knowledge move, not randomly but often with only the
vaguest associations behind their modulations until all impressions merge in a total composition.

Why then does Fitzgerald return to the discredited ordering
principle of chronology? As if his painstaking B-A-C time scheme
were almost an accident, he writes more than four years after
publication: "It's great fault is that the true beginning—the
young psychiatrist in Switzerland—is tucked away in the middle
of the book." [3] Since overtones of order and coherence are
drowned out by the dissonances of the ending in *Tender Is the
Night*—its fade-out of Diver disintegrated, psychiatrist become
mere particle, dislocated in a blanker and blanker time and space
—can Fitzgerald be trying to persuade us and himself that his
world or ours is one of order, clarity, harmony, or coherence?

[2] Ford Madox Ford, *Joseph Conrad: A Personal Remembrance* (Boston:
Little, Brown, 1924), pp. 136–37.
[3] Turnbull, ed., *Letters of F. Scott Fitzgerald*, p. 281.

Can he possibly think it his responsibility to make form an agent of propaganda for such a wishful vision?

As with most questions, this one suggests its own answer. Through rearrangement Fitzgerald chose to confront readers with Diver's set of illusions. For Diver in 1917 certainly sees himself as a heroic figure; further, he sees his society capable of stability and cohesion if catalysts like himself will add scientific knowledge to those middle-class " 'good instincts,' honor, courtesy, and courage." Because Diver is both subject and object in the novel, because one stands identified with *and* detached from him, it may be fitting that our sense of his disintegration parallels, perceptually, that actual decline. To put the matter another way, it seems to me that chronology in *Tender Is the Night* purposefully mocks itself. As the revised arrangement moves from beginning to end, perspective, point of view, and perceptual method change continuously. Formally, the novel is a composite of different viewpoints and narrative modes; behind them chronology is a death's head, a skeleton which itself crumbles under techniques which dissolve time and personality. Notice that after grand announcements of dates in the first two books (*Case History* and *Rosemary's Angle*) we rarely know toward the novel's end what year, month, or even day is taking its course. For the novel itself is a paradigm of that struggle waged between consciousness and history within its dramatic and reflective worlds.

Fitzgerald, I think, changed structures because he perceived historical context rather than impressionist form as the novel's unifying mode. There follow several convictions: that events impelling societies, cultures, nations, do have past and present dividing lines; that history does involve causes and effects; to understand how things happened may bring some freedom to present and future actions. Finally, I would suggest that history usually has starting points less arbitrary than consciousness and that for Dick Diver, as individual and as historical archetype, the "true beginning" is his journey to Europe, as mediator between two cultures (or, really, between nations in a larger culture). As an event, World War I, in *Tender Is the Night*, divides modern from Victorian culture. The war shelled a society to death, and in the wake of its chaos was born a period without order and morality or—and here lies the real distinction—without pretense to those values. Fitzgerald, then, begins with Diver at that point, so we see him as full of illusions of innocence as was the American nation—see him, like America, a half-unconscious ally in the war and the new order that was coming into being.

The revised structure modulates more clearly the narrative keys necessary to develop Fitzgerald's theme. On each of its levels that theme seems to be the causes and effects, indeed the condition itself, of "the broken universe of the war's ending"— Dick Diver's characterization, much later, both of general chaos and that chaos of identity plaguing almost everyone in this novel's world. For in *Tender Is the Night* Fitzgerald renders and reflects on the break-up of an older world, of personality, of history, of form, and the coming of a new one-dimensional world of mere surfaces, a world in which depth and complexity of personality and history are qualities to be annihilated, a world without mystery or sensibility, a world of barbaric technology.

Such a theme and such a focus require forms which will show the old world and its illusions still seemingly intact, then record through people, culture, and circumstances the process of dissolution. Likewise, novelistic forms must create a new and discontinuous world to replace the old. Fitzgerald's division of *Tender Is the Night* into five distinct books brings the novel into close relation with T. S. Eliot's use of fragmented form in *The Waste Land*. No longer does coherence come about from causality or a sense of exact relation among parts, or between parts and the whole. In this sense coherence is lost, for the very notion of fragmentation assumes no necessary relation of part to a whole. Fragments no longer can be called parts of a structure in any sense of causal relatedness. Necessarily, they exist in separation, if not isolation. Eliot's aesthetic relates particulars not as elements causally bound in a whole but as particles whose relation depends upon particular and distinct perspectives.

Fitzgerald's revision strategy counterpoints the traditional focus on the individual from youth to maturity, with its implications of order, causality, and inevitability, against an aesthetic focus which fragments consciousness and annihilates individual and historical continuity. Since *Tender Is the Night* undercuts an idealist view of history and personality with one more phenomenologist in nature, probably it is essential that we, whose vision of reality will be complicated and deepened, expose ourselves to the mode and the substance of Dick Diver's initial expectations, his way of seeing himself and the world of circumstances. In this way we both share his experiences and come, gradually or quickly, to separate ourselves from his vision and its paralysis.

His personal crack-up weathered, Fitzgerald's change of heart about *Tender*'s "true beginning" came from his awareness that he was dealing with the relationship between faculties of sympathy and judgment or, to be tougher about it, with survival. It is exactly as an individual, able to be seen in the round, that Dick Diver is a historical archetype. Through him we recognize ourselves, and as he makes his way through the "imaginary woods" of fantasy we see around him the historical settlements of America. Right from the first page, we must have a world against which to view him other than the Riviera society he has created largely himself. Even as we set sail with Diver, we must know, a knowledge shored up with fragments and allusions, that there is a chronology and a causality to the American journey and no matter how accidental it may appear, there is, if we can find the log-book, an explanation for the course of American history.

four

Case History: Lies, illusions, and the education of consciousness

1

Where migration and exile have been external escapes from American history, their internal mechanism has been that process of illusion that leads a man away from history (his story) into fantasy. Recall that first "fabulous voyager" of our literature. Unable to face responsibility, Rip Van Winkle wandered away from society and stayed dreaming in the Catskills for twenty years. Not just twenty years of his own manhood, but the twenty years of revolution and transition, those birth years of the American republic. Even upon his return historical changes matter little to Rip; if anything, he'd rather be a subject under King George than a citizen having to choose between Burr and Jefferson. What matters to Rip is that his wife is dead and that, therefore, his transition from young man to old has been accomplished without grief or trauma, without any of the *pain* we associate with human maturity. What one worries about, however, is Washington Irving's artistic complicity with Van Winkle's fantasy. For in his story we have a memory gap. No one, not Rip, not even Washington Irving knows or will admit what happened during those twenty years. The changes all can see, but why they came about, how they came about, what they mean for the future, seems to concern no one.

Not so with F. Scott Fitzgerald in *Tender Is the Night*, where, counterpointing Diver's illusions, Fitzgerald's allusions fill up the memory gaps. Stubbornly lined up against Diver's own nostalgic visions are the tough facts of past and ongoing history. Throughout *Case History* Diver's "great expectations" come across in a chronicle mode of narration. "The foregoing has the ring of a biography, without the satisfaction of knowing that the hero, like Grant, lolling in his general store in Galena, is ready to be called to an intricate destiny. Best to be reassuring—Dick Diver's moment now began" (6). In this double narrative voice Fitzgerald pretends to uphold but in fact undercuts the chronological-heroic-historical vision of personality. The "reassurance" promised is denied, first by the very link to Grant, that notorious moral and political failure who, as Diver tells Abe North, "just invented mass butchery," then presided over the reformation of America in the image of Robber Baron. In the second place, Fitzgerald's reassurance that Diver's "moment now began" must be seen in the context of that first chapter to which it is coda, a chapter in which have been pitched and drafted the narrative tone and formal skeleton for all of *Case History*.

What we are made to see at the beginning of *Tender Is the Night* is a division between personality and history. For the most part tonalities themselves establish Diver's self-image as full of romantic promise, unmarked and unmarred by history.

> Most of us have a favorite, a heroic period in our lives and that was Dick Diver's (4).
>
> . . . twenty-six years old, a fine age for a man, indeed the very acme of bachelorhood (3).
>
> . . . he had no idea that he was charming, that the affection he gave and inspired was anything unusual among healthy people.
>
> "Lucky Dick, you big stiff. . . . You hit it my boy. Nobody knew it was there before you came along." . . .
>
> At the beginning of 1917, when it was becoming difficult to

find coal, Dick burned for fuel almost a hundred textbooks that he had accumulated; but only as he laid each one on the fire, with an assurance chuckling inside him that he was himself a digest of what was within the book. . . .

"—And lucky Dick can't be one of these clever men; he must be less intact, even faintly destroyed. If life won't do it for him it's not a substitute to get a disease, or a broken heart, or an inferiority complex, though it'd be nice to build out some broken side till it was better than the original structure" (4).

He knew, though, that the price of his intactness was incompleteness (5).

Personality has not yet fathomed history or clashed with circumstances. Purposefully, the external force of the American government, through its deferment policy, has kept Dick intact away from the war's trauma. His skillful explorations in a new profession give him an Emersonian sense of *self*-reliance; he will be a pioneer of consciousness. Yet the Diver who thinks himself above time and distinct from history at once holds the view, in however pat and contrived a way, that to be complete as a person, perhaps to be a human being, "he must be less intact, even faintly destroyed." He feels an unreality, if not an injustice, about his privileged immunity from the forces of chaos raging in the world. But if disintegration and fragmentation are crucial to maturity of self, then such a process, thinks Diver, must happen naturally, organically, from *life* itself rather than from such substitutes as disease, broken heart, or inferiority complex.

The distinction between life and life's particulars betrays Diver's romantic-heroic conception of experience. " 'The best I can wish you my child,' so said the Fairy Blackstick in Thackery's *The Rose and the Ring*, 'is a little misfortune' " (5). Only the most innocent, ahistorical sensibility can seriously entertain such a myth of fortune's ways. Diver's compartments, as his own life shows, impose false orders on experience. Disease, broken heart, inferiority complex—these are *life's* work. Diver's distinction implies that among the brave, the noble, the favored, circumstance attacks in ways more distinguished than physical, emotional, and psychic sickness. He seems not to see any relationship between personality and history. Thus the necessity of "life" destroying one, faintly or otherwise, may refer dually to his own escape from the war's immediate blood and upheaval and to that American tendency to disclaim ties to the past, to imagine life and history beginning all over again with each generation.

In contrast, it is necessary to identify the different perspective on self and history offered by Fitzgerald. To begin with, quite aside from his ironic characterization of Diver as "too valuable, too much of a capital investment to be shot off in a gun" (3), he places Diver in a clearly denoted historical setting—wartime Switzerland. Comparing that nation to an island, Fitzgerald relates its position to Diver's; essentially, Switzerland is a thing acted upon, itself a subject of the war. Fitzgerald distinguishes clearly between national myth (illusion by propaganda) and historical fact. Only, perhaps because the old life of Swiss finance proceeds so carefully, "no one had missed the long trains of blinded or one-legged men, or dying trunks, that crossed each other between the bright lakes of Constance and Neuchatel" (3). Vienna, Diver's refuge, too has become "old with death" (4).

Yet for the Swiss heart illusions of ferocity replace involvement in World War I. If posters will not communicate the "contagious glory of those days" (3), so be it. Unlike Americans the Swiss know the difference between talk of war and facts of war. "As the massacre continued the posters withered away, and no country was more surprised than its sister republic when the United States bungled its way into the war" (3). Stripped of illusion, history's wars involve *massacres* and *bungling*, an antiheroic language which Fitzgerald, not Diver, summons from the beginning in *Tender Is the Night*. Often dramas of action or impression in this novel are modulated by Fitzgerald's own reflections, similar to but less direct than those, say, of Tolstoi, in

War and Peace. The technical given in *Tender Is the Night* is that there may be in a novel a historical perspective through the reflective voice of the novelist. Fitzgerald interprets through allusions and reflections the assembled pieces of his novel, even though these are fragments with all the implied disorder. If one quarrels with this aesthetic, he quarrels irrevocably with *Tender Is the Night*, for in each version Fitzgerald relies upon an identical technique.

> Thesis—impression of a character about reality.
> Antithesis—counter-impression by the novelist.
> Synthesis—aesthetic response merging sympathy and detachment.

Really, when the sophistication is removed from Diver's viewpoint, his perspective comes perilously close to Rosemary's, though fuller because of its historical dimension.

Having heard Diver's sense of his innocent Adam's proprietary rights over the world, we have Fitzgerald's reflections. "Dick got up to Zurich on fewer Achilles' heels than would be required to equip a centipede, but with plenty—the illusions of eternal strength and health, and of the essential goodness of people— they were the illusions of a nation, the lies of generations of frontier mothers who had to croon falsely that there were no wolves outside the cabin door" (5). What is telling about Fitzgerald's observations is that modulation, backward into history, of illusions into lies. Such optimistic crooning—a witch's lullaby —as the frontier mothers did, had a direct relationship to the necessities of their lives. While husbands hunted food or Indians, or plunged to new frontiers on male expeditions, mothers lied to keep the children quiet. But whatever the urgencies, the lie is seen as a lie. This perhaps needn't trouble us. Not so the process of euphemism which followed.

But how and why do lies become illusions? When survival is at stake, a lie sometimes does particular work well, but when Fitzgerald brings to lies the continuity of generations, he changes both effect and context. Make lies continuous over generations, and they'll become basic to consciousness and become fixed myths. Magnify a mother's whisper that everything is all right, there are no wolves in the woods, magnify this lie over generations, and you've got an assertion about reality. Loosen the assertion from its particular context, and one makes an Emersonian denial of hostility and conflict, a denial of the power of circumstance. Such an attitude leads one to project his own illusions on to the world. Illusions—they include Diver's sexual and historical heroic—shape a brittle mold for personality. And, if nurtured too long, they leave no new arrangements open to the pieces of self shattered in the inevitable disillusionment.

Through juxtaposition Fitzgerald has created a multi-dimensional "intricate destiny" for Dick Diver. It is clear that the case history is primarily Diver's, not Nicole's, also clear that Diver's paralyzing division of self is triggered by a historical event far more rending (World War I) than any personal tragedy. Finally, comparing Diver to Grant (historically they're polar figures, for Grant presided over an age and culture in the throes of liquidation, an age now collapsed and needing a psychiatrist more than a general), Fitzgerald hints that—although "Dick Diver's moment now began"—this idealist too will end up a prisoner of forces over which he, because of first perception and then will, has no control, no shaping power. Like President Grant, Diver will put together in Nicole Warren the divided halves of America, and find the composite, when intact again, inclined to cast him into obscurity once more.

2

Without going into detail about Nicole—her schizophrenia seems clear-cut and simple; it is Dick's case that is complex—I would note the context of Devereux, her father-violator. Between Devereux Warren and Sid Warren, leisure-class inheritor and rugged founding father of this capitalist dynasty, there is enormous difference. Given his Diverian social and moral focus, Fitzgerald's conception of the Warren incest heightens the book's cultural context. For Nicole is not violated in any Faulknerian context of lust exploding the bounds of convention. Not from Sid Warren's Robber Baron world of plunder and spoil does the incest come. Rather, grandfather Warren's outlets were external; they had to be if he was to build a family empire upon alliance with European royalty. No, Nicole's violation articulates the buried desires of a leisure-class Victorian world, refined to a point, whose original vitality is exhausted and ingrown.

Terrible are Devereux Warren and the unconscious ambivalence of Victorian euphemism. " 'Now let's not pay any attention to anybody else this afternoon—let's just have each other" (18). For the idle young widower to mask the real context, then pretend to pretend that he and his adolescent daughter are playing at being lovers, turns the illusion into reality.

The fact that Diver is at "the very acme of bachelorhood" and that a woman is his necessity does not yet engage him. His focus is professional, and Fitzgerald contrasts Diver's ambition with Franz Gregorovius and his burden of ancestry:

"Now tell me about yourself and your plans."
"I've only got one, Franz, and that's to be a good psychiatrist —maybe to be the greatest one that ever lived" (22).

("I want to be one of the greatest writers who have ever lived, don't you?") [1]

"That's very good—and very American. . . . I stand here and I see Zurich—there is the steeple of the Gross-Munster. In its vault my grandfather is buried. Across the bridge from it, lies my ancestor Lavater, who would not be buried in any church. Nearby is the statue of another ancestor, Heinrich Pestalozzi, and one of Dr. Alfred Escher. And over everything there is

[1] Fitzgerald, as quoted by Edmund Wilson in "Thoughts on Being Bibliographed," *Princeton University Library Chronicle* (February, 1944), p. 54.

always Zwingli—I am continually confronted with a pantheon of heroes" (22).

"Confronted" and, one might add, crippled. As Diver says at another time, Franz's merit, his competence comes "because fate selected you for your profession before you were born" (29). This past, continous, linked to a common place, a clear cultural identity, is the antithesis of schism between past and present, the migration and exile which make Fitzgerald's Americans uprooted souls. On the contrary, Franz's heritage can both circumscribe and give tough, substantial roots to personality. "Proud" and "fiery," Franz derives inner authority from the close physical, psychological, and cultural presence of his ancestors. "Sheeplike," his "pantheon of heroes" seems to dispossess him of contact with his own generation and to discourage him from the risks required by the intellectual life.

Diver looks out to more abstract forces to confirm his ambitious identity; " 'How's that for a government on the grand scale that knows its future great men?' " (22). As he explains his plans to Franz, Diver alludes to the American government's largesse, liquidations, and manifest-destiny view of the world. His illusion, however, that he is given leisure-class status (deferment, then officer rank, finally full pay for attendance at lectures) at no ultimate cost to himself, dovetails into the novel's major sociological irony. Certainly Diver's temporary privileged position dulls his awareness of the distinction between upperclass and middle-class societies and nurtures in him an illusion of invincibility.

> This was poor material for a socialist but good material for those who do much of the world's rarest work. The truth was that for some months he had been going through that *partitioning* of the things of youth wherein it is decided *whether or not to die for what one no longer believes.* In the dead white hours in Zurich staring into a stranger's pantry across the upshine of a street lamp, *he used to think that he wanted to be good, he wanted to be kind, he wanted to be brave and wise, but it was*

all pretty difficult. He wanted to be loved *too,* if he could fit it in (23, my italics).

What are these partitioned things if not the Prince Albert qualities of a Victorian gentleman? What but a white man's burden modified to serve one's own society? The "illusions of eternal strength and health, of the essential goodness of people" —these categorical assumptions refine into a contemporary code of chivalric service. "Used to," however, shows Diver's rejection, at least by his critical and historical faculties, of such a mode of behavior as real and living in his time. The question is whether or not to die for these genteel virtues, a question which American idealism evaded when it sent its willing young men out to die that the world might be made safe for democracy. They died, but democracy consisted of the political *partitioning* of defeated nations and of colonial nations. To put it another way, the question for Diver is whether, living by discredited, euphemistic values, to die as a person in a changed world of consciousness and circumstance. The pull of what Diver at his father's death will call the " 'good instincts,' honor, courtesy, and courage," follows primarily from fear of the unknown courses opened up to personality when standards of order and morality, thought to be necessary and absolute, wither away, and fragmentation and contingency become the dominant modes of being.

3

Within Diver's partitioned self, critical faculties, given method and evidence by psychiatry, oppose emotions inculcated by background and culture. At such a moment does Dick Diver encounter Nicole Warren. "Youth and beauty . . . a moving childish smile that was like all the lost youth in the world. . . . her face lighting up like an angel's" (25). Dick's impression of Nicole and the language he chooses to evoke her are particularizations of his general illusions. Yet he is aware of the facts of violation beneath the beauty. This sets up a delicate parallel between Nicole's beauty and violation and America's state of beauty and violation, particularly in the period between the Civil War and World War I. Then the continent had been violated, not only by war's necessities but by plundering expeditions and enterprises westward and by exploitation of human and natural resources. What compels us, with Dick, to Nicole and to America is the measure of legitimacy in his hope of relationship. Violation not yet having destroyed the beauty and integrity of woman or continent, why not a new equation or reformation, or, as the history books say, a Reconstruction? Yet reconstruction of woman or of nation will depend upon a sensitive balance of forces whose given must be an understanding of where the situation is at and why. The past, in short, must be known before it can be denied, not to mention reshaped in the present.

But beauty's trick has Dick create an almost abstract Nicole so that to his imagination she is more image of woman than woman. Contingencies of history and even of mortality are dissolved. "No background, no address," at last, "no breath." To be complete one must, as with Gatsby and Daisy, respond to the sexual-emotional attraction going on between these two people. Though he may sublimate, Diver does feel the "complementary vibration" which Nicole, even to the extent of *directing* her smile, desires him to feel. Fundamentally, however, Diver idealizes and fails to sensualize the sexuality between them.

In a reflection comparable in contrapuntal effect to his earlier account of Diver's illusions, Fitzgerald spells out his lover's ambivalence and abstraction. When Nicole asks him about a song, Dick answers: " 'Honestly, you don't understand —I haven't heard a thing' " (27). But Fitzgerald's voice, that of a Strachey-type biographer, echoes through the closed chambers of Dick's past. "Nor known, nor smelt, nor tasted, he might have added; only hot-cheeked girls in hot, secret rooms. The young maidens he had known at New Haven in 1914 had kissed men, saying 'There!' hands at the man's chest to push him away. Now there was this scarcely saved waif of disaster bringing him the essence of a continent" (27). The nightmare turn of the dream—woman and America as vampires—will recur in *Tender Is the Night* when even Tommy Barban, that "earnest Satan," will remark to Nicole on the sexual cannibalism he thinks peculiar to American women. Here, Dick is the victim of a repressive society in which sex too is partitioned. Because his energy and desire have been displaced by work, Nicole is less Nicole to him than she is the embodiment of his fantasy of perfect girl. In addition, she is metaphorically America. Young, violated, divided, evolving into a new relation between herself and the world, Nicole, in fact, parallels the nation. But for Diver, whose "illusions of eternal strength and health" are national as well as individual, Nicole embodies an America of dreams, a continent fully responsive to the twin promises of beauty and success.

In this same passage Fitzgerald introduces a horrifying, ideally incestuous dimension to the myth of woman (Eve) created by man (Adam). "Scarcely saved waif of disaster" suggests Nicole as orphan adopted by Dick. Psychologically, Eve has become daughter, not merely dream woman. Changed by her violation and her pain from rich young thing to fragile and promising human being, Nicole seems exactly what Diver's imagination would have been likely to create. Simultaneously Dick and Dr. Richard Diver—his authority as psychiatrist analogous to Devereux's actual fatherhood—Diver is able to be lover and protector. How better to fulfill the perfect male fantasy than to have wife and daughter in the same person?

Whatever Diver's mere image of her, Nicole Warren is a person in her own right. Tremblingly, her polarity swings between the image of herself as the young Ophelia and as the system's most "valuable property" and therefore as horse-trader out to add to her wealth. Her temptation is not ideal like Diver's but the material one of her Robber Baron fortune. But such an inheritance consists of more than money; it confers also on its possessor the capacity for tough-minded, even brutally practical judgments. One attains and preserves fortunes by knowing the market value of all things in the system, ultimately and perhaps first of all the value of oneself. Illness, however, brings to Nicole a dimension of sensibility. For an interval she too denies her past, but admirably and with complexity. She will not confuse love with property value. She will not lure one for whom she cares into those "Victorian side-chambers" which bred her violation and madness. She will confront the "emptiness and pain" of her evolving self.

But Dick, who had expected to be freed from this dubious, illogical affair, finds himself "metallic" and discontent, his very self without reference point. Like the clinic and like the broken, transitional world, he hovers "between being centripetal and centrifugal" (38). Lost within, he takes the first of many trips to find roots for his identity—a foundation for his life.

4

On the center of the lake, cooled by the piercing current of the Rhone, lay the true center of the Western World. Upon it floated swans like boats and boats like swans, both lost in the nothingness of the heartless beauty (40).

Geneva—centripetal spot in the Western world; pulpit of John Calvin, that Trotsky of the Reformation; birthplace in a major way of that Western culture climaxed by World War I. Yet if this passage evokes historical-theological origins and continuity, at the same time its objects call in doubt the nature of reality and knowledge. "Swans like boats and boats like swans." Which is it? Often names are a buffer between consciousness and reality. So, as we've seen with Diverian and American illusions, is language. As it continues, Fitzgerald's observation further mocks certainty and knowledge, no matter how consistent internally. For no matter what Diver calls those objects a mile below his funicular, both are "lost in the heartless beauty." There exists a reality, a beauty, a form beyond man's systems, a reality open to human consciousness, not subject to it. So that, as Diver wanders in and out of social frameworks, there is no comfort from the nonhuman universe. Although the natural and elemental world often reflects human contexts in *Tender Is the Night,* behind the human drama Fitzgerald presents nature as a background oblivious to and distinct from man, at least metaphysically. Nature is there, but usually its very form intensifies the chaos within Diver.

Confronted by Nicole in the mountains, briefly beyond social contexts, Diver assumes a role different from that of the psychiatrist or the male. Dick, however, discovers a different Nicole than the child he goes into the night to look for. His response calls to his mind his father, the Victorian clergyman: " 'You're teasing yourself, my dear. Once I knew a man who fell in love with his nurse—.' The anecdote rambled on, punctuated by their footsteps. Suddenly Nicole interrupted in succinct Chicagoese: 'Bull!' " (46). With one word she sensitizes his genteel skin. Despite Diver's training, they are essential and naked before each other. Desperate, at first Diver invokes to himself the past horror. "Short of anarchy he could not think of any chance that Nicole Warren deserved" (47). But he yields the self-righteous tone to actual changes. "There were now no more plans than if Dick had arbitrarily made some indissoluble mixture, with atoms joined and inseparable; you could throw it all out but never again could they fit back into the atomic scale" (47). "All changed, changed utterly"—and violently.[2] The intensity and newness of this experience compel Diver's being. Minutes before, he had believed in his mask of paternal Victorian counselor; now "he was thankful to have an existence at all,

[2] W. B. Yeats , "Easter 1916," *The Collected Poems of W. B. Yeats* (New York: Macmillan, 1956), p. 178.

if only as a reflection in her eyes" (47). All of his convictions about essential personality dissolve away in this new solution of elements. Nicole, whom he has cast as the violated child, has fought it out with him, not on any implicit, genteel level, but on an explicit, sexual level. Thus, for Diver, the problem of existence becomes how to reconcile one's past with the intense changes of ongoing experience.

As psychic historian, Fitzgerald creates another context beyond that of the lovers. The event parallels the disruptive, reverse metamorphosis going on within individuals and within the world generally in the "broken universe of the war's ending" (263).

> Suddenly there was a booming from the wine slopes across the lake; cannons were shooting at hail-bearing clouds in order to break them. The lights of the promenade went off, went on again. Then the storm came swiftly, first falling from the heavens, then doubly falling in torrents from the mountains and washing loud down the roads and stone ditches; with it came a dark, frightening sky and *savage* filaments of lightning and *world-splitting* thunder, while *ragged, destroying* clouds fled along past the hotel. Mountains and lake disappeared—the hotel crouched amid *tumult, chaos, and darkness* (48, my italics).

No reality, no perspective is permanent. Like the atom-splitting nuclear bomb, this "world-splitting," though elemental, is precipitated by human will and invention. No gods, no accidental fate decree this storm, only man's cannons in order to save the wine harvest. Apocalyptically, the storm repeats the creation between Dick and Nicole of a reality in which old forms and sureties have no more force. The anarchy of each event sets in motion energies far more uncontrollable and unpredictable than the original intention. The question is what life, what history will result from the "tumult, chaos, and darkness"? Does the hotel's crouch tell us that human society can survive the anarchy and madness of the twentieth century only by modes of bestiality?

The relationship between Dick and Nicole is finalized the next day by events over which Dick, given his allegiance to genteel manners, has no control, and over which Baby Warren exercises only an ironic control. For although Baby "wanted to use him innocently as a convenience" (50), for Dick and Nicole the actual train ride to Zurich is a metaphor for their life together. We think we have seen Dick Diver's moment begin, but in the background remains that allusion to General Grant whose moment ended at the beginning of his presidential alliance with America's material interests. In *Case History's* ending Fitzgerald only slightly implies the wider context; the emphasis is on the personal relationship, the facts of violation and madness, and the hope, both real and illusory, that a full and sensuous relationship may overcome them. But, as with Grant's reconstructed union, the bitterest irony of all is that schizophrenia, individually for Nicole, historically and collectively for America, will be changed into a new wholeness of money, metallic personality, and imperial values; a wholeness of one dimension, without complexity.

five

Rosemary's Angle: Beauty and terror—the spell of artifice

1

The struggle between Rosemary Hoyt's narrow-angle perspective and Fitzgerald's cultural reflections signifies many oppositions: romance versus history; stereotype versus personality; entertainment versus art. Although Fitzgerald adapts cinematographic techniques—wide-angle and close-up shots, frozen and fluid images in stills or moving frames, time halted and time wound up—to the novel, he brings to such artifice a complex critical moral and historical vision missing from the film in his time:

> I saw that the novel, which at my maturity was the *strongest and supplest medium for conveying thought and emotion from one human being to another*, was becoming subordinated to a *mechanical* and communal art that, whether in the hands of Hollywood merchants or Russian idealists, was capable of reflecting only the tritest thought, the most obvious emotion. It was an art in which words were subordinate to images, *where personality was worn down to the inevitable low gear of collaboration.*[1]

As Dick Diver watches Rosemary make *The Grandeur That Was Rome*, Fitzgerald, having commented upon the bravery

---

[1] F. Scott Fitzgerald, *The Crack-Up*, ed. Edmund Wilson (New York: New Directions, 1945), p. 78. My italics.

and industry of the movie profession, reflects that its people "were risen to a position of prominence in a nation that for a decade had wanted only to be entertained" (231). Clearly, he brings Rosemary to the novel's forefront during the interval from June to July, 1925, because he wishes to identify and question the direction of national experience and sensibility. For Rosemary Hoyt is no Isabel Archer; like the nation to which her face and gestures—her *talent*—panders, she wishes "only to be entertained." Experience matters not because of what it is, what it does, not because of how it feels, but because of how it looks and projects. Rosemary simultaneously creates and is created by a culture given mass allegiance through the common denominator of the movies.

The movies themselves mirrored and legitimized that "Return to Normalcy" after America's seeming commitment to crusade in World War I. For thoughts on the representative cultural nature of that haywire motion from "Normalcy" to "Boom," I turn to Erik Erikson:

> Men, especially in periods of change, are swayed by alternating world moods which seem to be *artificially created by the monopolists and manipulators of an era's opinions*, and yet could not exist without the highly exploitable mood cycles inherent in man's psychological structure. The two most basic alternating moods are those of carnival and atonement: the first gives license and leeway to sensual enjoyment, to relief and release at all cost; the second surrenders to the negative conscience which constricts, depresses, and enjoins man for what he has left unsolved, uncared for, unatoned.[2]

As American culture from 1919 to 1925 is reflected in *Tender Is the Night*, Erikson's alternating moods operate not distinctly or exclusively, but schizophrenically. What we see is the carnival mood dominating custom and experience, but not consciousness. The atoning, introspective psyche seems always to

[2] Erik H. Erikson, *Young Man Luther* (New York: W. W. Norton, 1958), p. 75. My italics.

be peering from behind the mask of gaiety. Conditions "unsolved, uncared for, and unatoned" inspire the desperate party, which is why Dick Diver tries, without success, to program his "carnivals of affection" out of life into art. So completely have these people cut off their desires from social purpose and humane values that they cannot face the trauma of self-recognition which would tell them that whether "unsolved and uncared for," or, solved and cared for, self and history are together.

"The uncertainties of 1919 were over—there seemed little doubt about what was going to happen—America was going on the greatest, gaudiest spree in history and there was going to be plenty to tell about it":[3]

> When the police rode down the demobilized country boys gaping at the orators in Madison Square, it was the sort of measure bound to alienate the more intelligent young men from the prevailing order. *We didn't remember anything about the Bill of Rights* until Mencken began plugging it, but we did know that such tyranny belonged in the jittery little countries of South Europe. If goose-livered business men had this effect on the government, *then maybe we had gone to war for J. P. Morgan's loans after all.*[4]

>> Palmer Raids
>> Sacco-Vanzetti
>> Re-*Birth of a Nation*
>> MOBS (lynch) GREET RETURNING SOLDIERS (black)
>> Ku Klux Klan
>> Prohibition
>> Teapot Dome

"The whole golden boom was in the air—its splendid generosities, its outrageous corruptions and the torturous death struggle of the old America in prohibition."[5] As Fitzgerald's

---

[3] Fitzgerald, *The Crack-Up*, p. 87.
[4] *Ibid.*, p. 13. My italics.
[5] *Ibid.*, p. 87.

fireworks imagery seems to imply, the very name for this interval—*boom*—connotes combustion and explosion, finally, disintegration. One has to see, as Fitzgerald saw, that the Diver
Riveria carnival was an abdication of human responsibilities,
as perhaps any regime in exile is an abdication. "One could get
away with more on the summer Riviera, and whatever happened
seemed to have something to do with art." [6] In its license the
American carnival evaded history, society, and personality.

Once but not for all, the aftermath of World War I showed
that mere American power could not improve either the world
or its own people. Either we supplied a new democratic vision
and policy or those visions back of World War I's massacre
would be superimposed upon our power. From Rosemary's
angle, with the movies' "glittering, grosser power" for compass,[7]
Fitzgerald anatomizes this abrupt interval whose charade, it
briefly appeared, might hold history at bay. Whose impressions
could more truthfully evoke this cultural moment than those of
Rosemary Hoyt, Hollywood "carnival" girl "embodying all the
immaturity of the race" (130)? Unlike the cast she briefly
performs with on the Riviera, untroubled by the opposing mood
of dispossession and depression, Rosemary's role is not to create,
but to pretend, to reassure the audience so that they'll continue
to respond with money and applause enough to keep the show
going. But Fitzgerald's role as moral historian in *Rosemary's
Angle* resembles the lion tamer's. It falls to him to alert the
audience that several of the lions have escaped from their cages.

2

As if to underscore the changed structure of power,
Fitzgerald begins *Rosemary's Angle* with the ritual of Diver asking for Nicole's hand in marriage. Only, *Baby* Warren stands in

[6] *Ibid.*, p. 19.
[7] *Ibid.*

for Devereux, the missing father, and her metaphor for marriage is the transfer of property. At once her capitalist magnate's scrutiny of Dick unveils the chasm between their two backgrounds:

"I'm a doctor of medicine. My father is a clergyman, now retired. We lived in Buffalo and my past is open to investigation. I went to New Haven; after that I was a Rhodes Scholar. My great-grandfather was Governor of North Carolina and I'm a direct descendent of Mad Anthony Wayne" (53).

Then the Warrens:

They were an American ducal family without a title—the very name written in a hotel register, signed to an introduction, used in a difficult situation, caused a psychological metamorphosis in people, and in return this change had crystallized her own sense of position (53-54).

From Mad Anthony Wayne, revolutionary general, then explorer and Indian fighter, to one more genteel clergyman, and, last, to Diver himself, the end of the line, the progression away from fame and power of the Diver clan contrasts with the gathering force and prominence of the Warrens, whose present position is overwhelming enough to make its shady past closed to investigation. Beyond these contrasts there may be a telling American resemblance; for it may be that ancestral violence subtly exhausts the independence of a clan's descendants, especially if the original violence is dubious enough to spawn familial guilt.

In any case Nicole Warren's mind and values are the only reference points in an interior monologue that renders the Diver's marriage until the arrival of Rosemary in June, 1925. Far from her past sense of no self, she develops an almost narcissistic preoccupation with her self: "Sitting on the stanchion of this life-boat *I* look seaward and let my hair blow and shine. *I* am motionless against the sky and the boat is made to carry my form onward into the blue obscurity of the future, *I* am Pallas Athene carved reverently on the front of a galley" (55, my italics). "Life-boat" becomes "galley," whose cargoes, whether won in battle or haggled for in strange marketplaces, were rowed by slaves. In any case Pallas Athene signifies the myth of male as sole progenitor (Adam dreaming, then waking to find Eve created from his body) in classical culture. Not only did this daughter spring from Zeus, but she became in her own right battle-goddess, protectress of civilization and the city. Not only does Nicole indulge in self-worship, but she conceives of herself as goddess, a role she will fulfill later with Tommy Barban as their calculated sexuality announces a barbaric civilization. Here her self-absorption and identification with a legendary goddess underlines her (and Diver's) rootlessness. Having flown past continuities, having no home, they move from one wonder of the world to another. Relation to place seems momentary and superimposed; relation to society—there is none.

"Talk is men," she thinks and goes on to spell herself as the series of men in her life. External being consists solely of masculine presences. Knowledge, and articulation of that knowledge, belongs to men. Nicole conceives of herself as now one man, now another, or as composite of different male personalities. For her the female world is a silent world—one however which internalizes patterns of history and society. What men and the world may be in their own right is antithetical to Nicole Warren's therapeutic state of being.

Nicole, even as refraction of whatever persons and conditions impinge on consciousness, presides over a domain of fortune and power over human situations. Through her interior monologue Fitzgerald has rendered Nicole's gradual flight from pain and her ascent to the Olympus of a Pallas Athene. The irony is that all has been pieced together by Dick Diver for love and protection of Nicole with Warren resources seeming incidental still. But so careful has been his arrangement that its motive and urgency remain concealed from Nicole as she founds her self upon this world.

3

What is to be investigated is the post-Victorian, Edwardian world presided over by a nouveau leisure class after the partial eclipse of old aristocracies in World War I. Through close-ups overlayed with panorama (history conferred on the scene), Fitzgerald shows the conflicts between that "world all put together . . . by the gray-haired men of the golden nineties" (190) and a contemporary world driven mad and centerless by the wounds of the war and the Russian Revolution. Though its media are words and images, Fitzgerald's aesthetic at the beginning of *Rosemary's Angle* is cinematographic. We see the social world as a moving stage, its characters as a cast of actors and a director (Diver). It's as if a camera with a far-sighted lens sweeps over the Riviera disclosing nature and the evolving, dissolving human scene (old villas rotted like so many water lilies). The technical symmetry between *Case History* and these opening shots of the Riviera is marked. There we were introduced not simply to Dick Diver and his pattern of illusions but to the facts and conditions of self and war. Just so, we do not here see only what Rosemary Hoyt sees; we see a reality not included in her version of the world. Fitzgerald's camera takes in "the distant image of Cannes, the pink and cream of old fortifications, the purple Alp that bounded Italy" (58). But soon life is restricted to services performed for the sleeping leisure class.

Onto this Riviera stage, untrained for it, walks Rosemary Hoyt. As did Dick Diver in Vienna eight years before, Rosemary radiates innocence, of herself and of historical circumstances. She was "nearly complete, but the dew was still on her" (59). Edenic in tone, the image makes clear that Rosemary is a child, not a woman. She lives apart from the world; she will need initiation into it and into her own womanhood. As she looks over the beach and its people, she gradually translates the activity into a metaphor close to her experience: "After a while she realized that the man in the jockey cap was giving a quiet little performance for this group" (61). From this point of recognition forward Diver and his circle seem but extensions of her professional mask.

So Rosemary, who has prospered into a celebrity exactly because she can deal with reality as a controlled set and life as a production, will enter the Diver world seemingly on her own terms. At home with the resemblances, she does not recognize the distinction between her professional movie-acting and the private drama of the Divers' circle. The latter enterprise, with Dick as director, has assumed the dramatic mask for survival's sake. On still another level, also unperceived by Rosemary, movie-acting seduces a nation away from psychological and historical realities and, like Diver's performances, into a territory of illusions where order and sanity are achieved, *finally*, by the happy ending. After suitable perils, for instance, *Daddy's Girl* celebrates the triumph in action of the "illusions of a nation"; also of course the fantasies of a nation. Rather Rosemary sees all action as gratuitous acting, as confident exhibition of personality. In her psychological infantilism, it does not seem that individuals might have to create masks in order to conceal personality from circumstances too painful to be borne, or from thoughts too disruptive to be allowed to linger in the mind. It does not occur to her that personality sometimes can be too frail for its own desires or the world's circumstances. As long as she can see the Riviera as a set, its inhabitants and events as actors and scenes, then her innocent, optimistic self can be confident that whatever resolutions there are in this society will be sophisticated versions of *Daddy's Girl's* happy ending—father still protector, daughter voyeuristically violated, but physically intact. In short, she does not understand her movie's relation to the world. Even if she knew Nicole's mystery, she would not be able to see that she, as heroine of *Daddy's Girl,* came to fame by participation in a horrifying euphemistic fantasy of the Warren incest.

Characteristically, Rosemary cannot approach the substance of French life or culture or the history of past epochs and empires breathed forth from the dust of monuments, mansions, and orthodox churches. Being an American heroine has created in Rosemary a susceptibility to formulas. "Accustomed to seeing the starkest grotesqueries of a continent heavily underlined as comedy or tragedy," she is "untrained to the task of separating out the essential for herself" (70). Given history's existence, this means she has no perspective from which to view history save the debased fairy-tale bits and pieces found in mass magazines. For Rosemary even French newspaper headlines are unreal; only the word-movies in *Le Temps* and *The Saturday Evening Post* are real.

But what starkly pinpoints Rosemary's indulgence in antihistorical romance are the novel's opposing visions of pre-Revolution Russia. She finds vividly alive the memoirs of an exiled Russian princess, but her sentimental failure of perception leaves it to Fitzgerald to introduce, with that poignance and finality of his historical references, the actual fate of the Russian royalty and nobility: "Most of all there was the scent of the Russians along the coast—their closed book shops and grocery stores. Eleven years before when the season ended in April, the door of the Orthodox Church had been locked and the sweet champagnes they favored had been put away until their return. 'We'll be back next season,' they said, but this was premature, for they were never coming back any more" (71). Some things, therefore, are final beyond all fantasy, all contingency, all shifts in point of view. War and revolution annihilated this aristocracy, and similar cataclysms hang over their Western survivors, however unaware these new ducal families may be of the spreading chaos.

Inevitably, she turns to Diver because "he was all complete

there" (75), because, perhaps in his weariness with the director's role, he can make her forget that human relations are dramas. In addition, Rosemary responds to Diver because her virtues—"self-control and self-discipline" (75)—are his virtues. To be brief, Rosemary chooses Dick because he is the male platonic conception of herself. Her related wish *to be created* as his female self is realized with "her sense that Dick was taking care of her, and she delighted in responding to the eventual movement as if it had been an order" (77). One can, without bogus psychoanalysis, connect this passivity to her military upbringing, a background which her career as actress has reinforced with director replacing officer-father.

If Rosemary's eyes film the Divers, then Fitzgerald's reflections subtitle their situation, one in which changes are concealed from the newcomer by the seemingly stable, static ritual of their lives. Externally, their culture appears one of free, and at the same time, perfected social forms, a culture to which money and sophistication have granted an aesthetic beauty and class. But, internally, and in the mere curiosity of the rituals, a "qualitative change [has] already set in" (77); and, in an over-all way, Fitzgerald's perspective implies that the very givens, the sought-after conditions of leisure-class existence, turn the wheel of its dissolution. That same polarity, for instance, between democratic promises and aristocratic rigidity which had sustained the nineteenth-century upper classes had brought about their collapse in Russia. And, generally, World War I, in Fitzgerald's historical vision, marks the point of no return for Western Protestant civilization, whose roots lay in the Reformation and its ensuing economic and psychic journey beyond Europe. As an event, the war both signaled and began to bring about what Oswald Spengler soon called the decline of the West: migrations back over the ancient empires, this time with no destinations; absentee money with less and less connection to its sources; middle classes unincorporated, either devoured or sent down the ladder toward a more and more nonexistent peasantry; old sureties (nationalism and religion) less and less able to hold the masses in bondage. How long could these suffice the old orders that are left?

4

There is in this novel a changing relation between beauty and artifice. In contrast to the spell cast on Rosemary by the autonomous, artificial world of the studio, Nicole, alone in her garden, experiences her environment in sensuous tranquility. The moment is created not through dramatic or reflective or symbolic language, but by developing a truly moving-picture of experience. "She walked on, between kaleidoscopic peonies massed in pink clouds, black and brown tulips and fragile mauve-stemmed roses, transparent like sugar flowers in a confectioner's window—until, as if the scherzo of color could reach no further intensity, it broke off suddenly in mid-air, and moist steps went down to a level five feet below" (82–83). The experience, in its several modes of sensation, fuses for Nicole the aesthetic and the orgiastic. These elements come together through a language of successive images exploding in motion, rather than language whose effect is clearly measured through definition, whose meanings are planed off. As a woman, Nicole shuns language, certainly language as a social, purposeful instrument. Privileged creator of this multidimensional garden—"five small houses had been combined to make the villa and four destroyed to make the garden" (83)—Nicole cannot but be reminded of her history's power and burden even by the fluid beauty of this private garden.

Back on the stage of social convention, one wonders to what extent Diver gives the parties for Nicole's sake, and to what extent they are displacements of his constructive activity in the world. For Diver's role as priest and pope of these parties and this leisure-class society begins to take on a demonic cast: " 'I want to give a really *bad* party. I mean it. I want to give a party where there's a brawl and seductions and people going home with their feelings hurt and women passed out in the cabinet de toilette' " (84). Diver is kidding, calling attention, of course, to the grace and charm and communion of his parties. One can see, though, how such fantasies of chaos could result from his habitual commitment to order and self-discipline. For no matter how exquisite his parties, their relation to Diver will be determined by the quality and purpose of his life generally. As *the* events in his life, parties expose that vacuum created by the gradual abandonment of his career. Not only Nicole, who is externally responsible, but Diver himself realizes that his "excitement about things has reached an intensity out of proportion to their importance" (84).

Through subtle metaphors, Fitzgerald superimposes a context upon Dick's uneasiness:

> The reaction came when he realized the waste and extravagance involved. He sometimes looked back with awe at the *carnivals of affection* he had given, as a *general* might gaze upon a *massacre* he had ordered to satisfy an *impersonal blood lust* (84, my italics).

Compare General Grant's memoirs:

> While a battle is raging one can see his enemy mowed down by the thousand, or the ten thousand, with great composure; *but after the battle these scenes are distressing,* and one is naturally disposed to do as much to alleviate the suffering of an enemy as a friend.[8]

As drama yields to naked reality, one's skin of detachment sloughs to reveal the guilt beneath. The metaphor changes from one disingenuously close to the parties' surfaces—"carnivals of affection"—to one charged with murder and guilt. What the comparison's logic suggests is that ultimately Diver's parties waste energy, spoil emotions, and destroy personality. Given his

8 *Personal Memoirs of U. S. Grant* (New York: Charles L. Webster, 1886) vol. 1, p. 521. My italics.

heroic illusions and his actual relationship with the world, Diver's need "to satisfy an impersonal blood lust" arises from frustration at his own "waste and extravagance," frustration at a life in which his earlier instinct toward discovery and application of clinical theory has been distorted until his profession is director of social drama on a leisure-class stage. If I, he seems to say, am wasteful, extravagant, and trivial with myself and my energies, let the norm for all who enter my world be waste, extravagance, and triviality. Like Grant, Diver, on the bloodless (only for the time being) battlefield of the Riviera, can work his will both ways. First, this outsider enjoys the luxury of command, then, psychic massacre ended, he can use guilt and melancholy to seem to join the race of mortals, though in inner as well as outer intensity he feels himself a hero.

Yet for this particular dinner party Fitzgerald through Diver creates an experience that, briefly, is more spontaneous than contrived, more aesthetic than social or psychological. For a moment one connects the metaphor of drama and stage (dinner table even becomes "like a mechanical dancing platform" [91]) with Yeats's attempt in "A Prayer for My Daughter" to combat history's madness and brutality with an aesthetic vision of society:

> How but in custom and in ceremony
> Are innocence and beauty born?
> Ceremony's a name for the rich horn,
> And custom for the spreading laurel tree.[9]

Events past and to come as well as the inner condition of the Divers mark this evening as an interval in time and space, uncharted by continuities until Nicole's lapse into chaos.

Naively, Rosemary perceives the occasion's singularity. Once more a camera lens, her eyes focus on the Villa Diana not merely as a splendid place, but as the "center of the world." And she

9 W. B. Yeats, "A Prayer for My Daughter," *The Collected Poems of W. B. Yeats* (New York: Macmillan, 1956), p. 192.

is included, primarily as audience, minimally as actress. So far hers is a bit part, but director Diver may make her a star—if he will fall in love with her. So that we have a stage—presumably a *stage* depends more upon personality, upon the actors themselves than does, to Rosemary, a *set* which relies more upon legerdemain of camera and props—and Rosemary's inkling that "some memorable thing" will happen. That surprise, she seems to think, will come forth from the evening itself. Rosemary is utterly wrong; Nicole's sudden epilepsy has deep roots in the past. The Villa Diana stage setting should prevent such relapses, but it does not. Quite simply, Rosemary's dramatic framework of "some memorable thing" directly contradicts the party's motive and form.

Diver does have in mind a memorable atmosphere. But whatever drama there is should rest with him; from the rest it should be concealed, minimal and accidental, if not nonexistent. What we see are Diver's psychological gifts working not professionally, but socially. Not rationally but magically, not the couch but the dinner table frees these diverse people, each from his or her neurotic inclination. Indeed, the freedom conferred both by the natural beauty of the night and by the elegant beauty of lanterns and outdoor dinner table leads these people, individually, separately, toward a certain oneness. Party becomes gathering; socially, the whole surpasses the sum of its parts.

Through all this we are discouraged from merely following the circle of Rosemary's "romantic eyes" (96). "Rosemary, as dewy with belief as a child from one of Mrs. Burnett's vicious tracts, had a conviction of homecoming, of a return from the derisive and salacious improvisations of the frontier" (91). Here are Diver's "illusions of eternal strength and health, and of the essential goodness of people—the illusions of a nation" (5). America becomes identified with strident, scornful, prurient behavior; unconsciously, Rosemary indulges in the orphan fantasy. Child stolen (by the Indians?) from the log cabin is now transported to aristocratic fairyland. Of course Rosemary's "dewy belief" and its Riviera actualization both have their reference point in the "salacious improvisations" (should we say brutality and barbarity?) of a frontier owned, exploited, and now extended to Europe by Sid Warren and his descendants.

No longer is Rosemary alone; for an interval no one can distinguish *seems* from *is*. "The table seemed to have risen a little toward the sky like a mechanical dancing platform, giving the people around it a sense of being alone with each other in the dark universe, nourished by its only food, warmed by its only lights" (91). Without exception the guests are drawn too far into the illusion to notice how it is achieved, or to notice its very limited reality in time and space. And, as we shall discover very explicitly later on in *Rosemary's Angle*, far from being nonexistent, these other things and beings in the universe have themselves made possible this illusion because they have paid "a tithe to Nicole" (113) and the Warren family dynasty.

Though instantaneous, this moment is continuous. Though stationary, it is expansive. Spontaneously "the two Divers began suddenly to warm and glow and expand, as if to make up to their guests . . . for anything they might still miss from that country left well behind" (91). The framework is social, the process spontaneous and staged, but the metaphor of a newly discovered world, never before intruded upon and with its reality of wholeness among personalities, recalls the loss of self-consciousness and the discovery of a rich unknown that takes place between lovers or between discoverers and a new continent. There follows too a closeness between this richness of personality and the elemental scene around and beyond the human drama, a relationship alluded to often in Fitzgerald's novels but usually realized out of some nostalgic desire for the past rather than from the dynamic contact with space in time present. Nature's effluence—that of the night and the Mediterranean below—seems transferred to the Divers' outdoor stage. "The magic left these things and melted into the two Divers and became part of them" (91). But magic is a fluid concept, carrying with itself a sense of enchantment limited to interval. The Divers don't really absorb and contain all reality's spirit; they only seem to. The illusion has momentarily leapt all physical and psychological boundaries of space and duration; it has become all-encompassing.

Abruptly, this communion dissolves, and "the rarer atmosphere of sentiment was over before it could be irreverently breathed, before they had half realized it was there" (91). The guests cease to be a gathering and change back into a cast of warring actors. Oblivious to their conversation's significance and "inwardly on fire" for Diver, Rosemary hears Barban and McKisco verbalize the conflict of values going on in the novel and in the twentieth century as it develops outside *Tender Is the Night*. McKisco, a sterile, cowardly, academic man, speaks for socialism and Berber nationalism, but the oppressed he defends can expect no active help from him. Barban, still a professional soldier, fights for property—his own and that of Europe and her empires generally. As will be true in their duel, these men deal with each other ritually. McKisco mistakenly (particularly in the emerging political context of the twenties and thirties) dismisses Barban as "the end product of an archaic world, and, as such, worthless" (92).

Here, Yeats's second coming upheavals of personality are fulfilled metallically:

> The best lack all conviction, while the worst
> Are full of passionate intensity.[10]

For Tommy Barban speaks and is willing to act on behalf of an ancient code of honor. In their aristocratic forms he embodies the three virtues passed on to Dick Diver by his clergyman father: "honor, courtesy, and courage." Barban is loyal enough to the Divers to silence gossip, loyal enough to rituals to force McKisco to act out his flip invocation of the code *duello*. It is,

[10] Yeats, "The Second Coming," *Collected Poems*, p. 185.

however, Barban who steals (or does he reclaim, recapture) the woman whose reputation he now upholds with such impeccable fierceness. At that future point Diver's reign as prince ends, but his was an interregnum from the start. Moreover, with Barban's usurpation (really accession) through magnetism of body and fortune, the Warren dynasty increases the scope and power of its empire.

During the crisis between McKisco and Barban, Diver appears, staves off a scene, then confers upon Rosemary what she feels is a time "earned" alone with him. Their encounter comes closer to being a duel, a subliminal contest of personalities, than the duel fought with pistols the next morning between Barban and McKisco. In Diver we witness a change from contingent sexual impulse to director's creation of a controlled dramatic situation. But the risk is too great, the warren which encloses him too closely surveyed. " 'You don't know what you want. You go and ask your mother what you want.' She was stricken. She touched him, feeling the smooth cloth of his dark coat like a chasuble" (95). The paternal jibe at once conceals and unveils the conflict between Diver's mind and desires, but it has an effect opposite to its intention. Rosemary sacramentalizes him; he is no longer merely or chiefly a man. In reverse, Dick has the king's touch. Rosemary, stricken into a religiously subliminal surrender, gives the illusion of falling to her knees. Her daughter role and Diver's paternal one mask the desire of each, just as the evening's social forms and aesthetic touches mask the pain and chaos going on within the afflicted persons.

5

As always in this novel, fantasy blurs reality; mind frightens self away from body. Rosemary's sexual imaginings evoke "America's Sweetheart," Mary Pickford's oft-repeated matinee dream of a first kiss. Disturbed by the directness of her erotic impulse, Rosemary "tried to think with her mother's

mind about the question" (97), which is ironically what Diver
had told her to do. But although Rosemary's reference point
is indeed her mother, Mrs. Speers's framework is one of amorality
and pragmatism, her metaphor a military one often applied to
sexuality, specifically, the metaphor of the duel. " 'Wound yourself or him—whatever happens it can't spoil you, because economically you're a boy, not a girl' " (98). The term "economically" exactly conveys the special sense in which Rosemary is
her own master (or mistress). Disappointment in love or not,
her career will go on; from it derives her essential strength:
" 'You were brought up to work—not especially to marry' "
(98). Mrs. Speers's remark inverts Rosemary and Dick Diver.
Rosemary will stick to the economic professional formula, whereas
Diver's heritage of service and the nonsatisfaction of his own desires has inclined him to a marriage which paralyzes both his
work and his sexuality. For, most of all, his career serves Nicole;
he lacks that "further departure" beyond what D. H. Lawrence
calls "the great sex goal." [11] Rosemary, on the other hand, uses
the "greater purpose" of her career to define herself, sexually, as
a woman. In any case, Fitzgerald does not sentimentalize sexual
identities; he does, however, show how thoroughly and danger-
ously economic realities influence one's womanhood or manhood,
particularly when a culture's work roles require men to project
the image of father and women that of perpetual girl.

Meanwhile, presiding over his party like a general, Dick
shifts the front to Paris. But his triumphs of gaiety come at a
heavy cost. It is as if the exigent supply lines—male energy
and direction—are, because of miscalculation, cut off from
Diver's female troops. A cavalier general, Diver absorbs the
burden to the point of physical and psychic exhaustion. What
such a man does not seem to understand is that his collapse
will cost those under his command at least an aspect of their
own humanity. It is as if—to apply the Adam and Eve myth im-

[11] D. H. Lawrence, *Psychoanalysis and the Unconscious and Fantasia of the
Unconscious* (New York: Viking Press, 1960), p. 220.

plicit in Diver's relationships—the man can create the woman, but that she, in the process, absorbs his strength and very being until, exhausted, he dies and she is free in her own right. The truth is that these women live in a world which, though created by their men, is created for the women and is a world antithetical to social and historical purpose and creation.

Marriage becomes a metaphor for male entropy. Energy flows to the wife and that incestuous social circle related to leisure and domesticity. Diver and North, unlike their Victorian prototypes, have no secret lives, either sexual or creative; their drama of dissolution (making nothing out of something) plays itself out entirely on female territory. Not that this is the women's fault. On the contrary, Diver unconsciously uses Victorian genteel values and forms to mask his failure actively to seek risks and satisfactions beyond the family. The fact that Nicole can become suddenly an emergency patient further dissipates his options. In any case there is no society beyond the wife, no world of action in which to play out neglected purpose or desire. Not, anyway, in these men's lives. Whatever infidelities they try are all the more guilt-ridden for their occurrence within the family's backyard.

Women in *Tender Is the Night* derive personal identity and association with America from those political and socio-economic metaphors chosen by Fitzgerald to render the American system. One way, for example, to differentiate between Rosemary and Nicole as individual women and as embodiments of America is to contrast their attitudes toward money and the things money can buy. Although each operates within a capitalist framework, their viewpoints recall the Marxist distinction between use value and exchange value. For middle-class Rosemary to spend money there must be direct relationship among price, object, and the particular work which, for her, has set this process in motion. Nicole, on the other hand, indulges in an almost abstract "wholesale buying" because she becomes a synecdoche not merely for America, but for the growing American world empire

—an empire which another world war will elevate to *the* world empire.

An embodiment of America, Nicole fuses Henry Adams's religious and industrial principles of energy. In America the dynamo serves Nicole Warren, a goddess (daughter and continent) violated by her protector (father and nation-builders), but still able to conceal this exploitation through a configuration —marriage, therapy, leisure society—made possible by the dynamo's exploits of energy.

> Nicole was the product of much ingenuity and toil. For her sake trains began their run at Chicago and traversed the round belly of the continent to California; chicle factories fumed and link belts grew link by link in factories; men mixed toothpaste in vats and drew mouthwash out of copper hogsheads; girls canned tomatoes quickly in August or worked rudely at the Five-and-Tens on Christmas Eve; half breed Indians toiled on Brazilian coffee plantations and dreamers were muscled out of patent rights in new tractors—these were some of the people who gave a tithe to Nicole and, as the whole system swayed and thundered onward, it lent a feverish bloom to such processes of hers as wholesale buying, like the flush of a fireman's face holding his post before a spreading blaze (114).

This gargantuan sentence, like the imperial process it describes, comprises many networks, each separate unless one traces and understands the grand design. The flatness of the opening statement should not deflect one's attention from the connection between Nicole and America, between the privileged beauty violated and then sacramentalized by the American system and those mechanical, increasingly self-propelling forces which continue to expand this technological, largely absentee imperial process. Vietnam, for instance, represents an exception to the new colonialsim, for success by the latter method should not require the direct participation of the empire nation. If our industrial missionaries can convert the natives to technology and excite in them a desire for immediate miracles, then they and the land itself will pay economic, political, and military tithes to American business and government in exchange for use of our sacramentals. Domestically, Nicole is supported not only by the system's exploitations, but also, Fitzgerald insists, by the awe of Rosemary. Rosemary's middle-class response to Nicole's wanton spending consists of the resolve that "presently she would try to imitate it" (114), an imitation which probably will increase geometrically the labor she, in turn, must give back to the system.

In America too Nicole's beauty gains luster from her violation. Puritanism, it seems, leads to fascination with sex, especially those acts that are most tabooed. Still beautiful, still worshipped by men, Nicole's mystery has subtly increased. What we are seeing historically, as Adams points out in "The Dynamo and the Virgin," is transference of energy idea-source from organic to mechanical, sexual to electrical, now nuclear power (perhaps the transfer is symbolically completed by Nicole's marriage to Barban). Yet Adams claims, speaking of all the aesthetic and social energy generated by the idea of the Virgin Mary, "this energy was unknown to the American mind. An American Virgin would never dare command; an American Venus would never dare exist." [12] Perhaps the process worked backwards in America. Maybe men, having denied women, made woman an inspiration after the facts of conquest and accumulation. But in *Tender Is the Night* woman become dynamo seems an appropriate form for the new empire's goddess. For Adams the virgin "was goddess because of her force; she was the animated dynamo; she was reproduction—the greatest and most mysterious of all energies." [13] But by the time of *Tender Is the Night* fecundity means system and empire. There is a certain "mysterious energy" engaged in the economic, social, and political processes that feed Nicole's fortune, which, like that energy released

[12] Henry Adams, *The Education of Henry Adams* (Boston: Houghton Mifflin, 1961), p. 385.
[13] *Ibid.*, p. 384.

by the medieval Virgin Mary, exceeds the idea's original intention. Perhaps in America violation has become the national mystery.

Because of Fitzgerald's last metaphor, the entire centrifugal process turns in upon Nicole and what is required for her own survival as an individual person. Fitzgerald's subtlety is his comparison between Nicole's "feverish bloom" and "the flush of a fireman's face." If the fireman does not rein in the flames, then the same "spreading blaze" whose energy warms and illuminates him may break its bounds and destroy him. Likewise, Nicole's bloom is "feverish," and therefore capable of eating away and finally consuming her whom it now nourishes. No matter how random and wanton it may appear, her luxury must be carefully organized; otherwise the whole process, personal and institutional, will rage out of control and sweep her to havoc along with the system. This metaphorical imperative for order becomes especially urgent in view of Nicole Warren's fragile margin of sanity.

Because of her Hollywood illusions about torrents of passion, Rosemary, in her own desire for Dick, does not see that Nicole's apparent indifference to her rendezvous with Dick is a subtle form of passion. For in reality Nicole's ritual buying, her lavishing of affection through gifts, prepares her for Dick. Granted the outrageous and far-reaching cost, it is her way of contributing to his dream of personality in order to come closer to him in love. Most unperceived by Rosemary is the fact that Nicole's love for Dick goes on inside her in a territory beyond drama, whereas Rosemary knows that her own chance of success with Diver must come from the angle of her career. As an actress who deals independently with the world, she objectifies Diver's search, first, for an innocence he has not enjoyed with Nicole and, second, for an escape from the narrowing circle of domesticity wherein his life has begun to turn—repetitively.

six

Casualties: The failure
of history is the
failure of consciousness

1

"We thrive by casualties. Our chief experiences have
been casual." So wrote Ralph Waldo Emerson in "Experience,"
the Emerson who, according to Santayana, "read transcenden-
tally, not historically, to learn what he himself felt, not what
others might have felt before him." [1] In this perceptual soil
causality must wither. If life and history are so many accidental
happenings, then the boomerang of responsibility has no just
target. A casualty's victim has no one to blame for his injury
but the condition of reality itself. Certainly Emerson's asser-
tions encourage acceptance of life's unpredictability and discourage reliance upon systems—legitimately. But the historian
cannot take casualties casually. Behind history's events, conditions, and oppressions, he must look for patterns and causes.
No matter how scrupulous his impartiality, a historian's arrangement of the facts will disclose assumptions about history and
the conduct of men.

In *Casualties* Dick Diver, historian once removed from Fitzgerald, struggles to conscious articulation of the complex cul-

[1] G. Santayana, *Winds of Doctrine* (New York: Charles Scribner's Sons,
1926), p. 192.

tural history responsible for those millions of World War I dead. But, tragically, a nostalgic sensibility inhibits his intelligence. In fact, his half-staged, half-spontaneous mourning fatally extends his own identity crisis to what Erikson might call a middle-aged, and therefore disastrous, "moratorium" on maturity.[2] For they are, most of these dead, distant from the burden of American history. "A penny for the old guy" here in France, so hopes Diver's unconscious, may keep any American spooks in the proper recess of his memory. Whatever the reason, the same man who mourns the dead of England, France, and Germany alike, and the passing of *his* "beautiful lovely safe world," the man Fitzgerald links with General and President Grant—this man will, when murder (caused by Abe North) touches his own life, dismiss it as " 'only some nigger scrap.' " Coupled with a paralytic Victorian sentimentality, how can this abdication of human responsibility, individual and historical, do anything else but sink Diver into a melancholy, guilty incapacity to change his world, his marriage, or even his own life?

The truth must be told. The roots of *Casualties* recede to the betrayal of humanity, black and white and red, in American history between the Civil War and its shameful sequel of Reconstruction:[3]

Emancipation Proclamation
"Forty Acres and a Mule"
Freedmen's Bureau
Freedmen's Bank Allowed to Bankrupt
Revolution of 1876—Suppression of Black Votes
Grandfather Clause

[2] Erik H. Erikson, *Young Man Luther* (New York: W. W. Norton, 1958), p. 43.
[3] Full discussion of the "Reconstruction" period in American history is found in *Black Reconstruction in America* (New York: Russell and Russell, 1935); and in Ch. 3 and 4 of *The Souls of Black Folk* (Greenwich, Conn.: Fawcett, 1961), both by W. E. B. DuBois.

"Atlanta Compromise"
Plessy v. *Ferguson*

Fitzgerald reveals the horrifying pattern as he weaves melo-dramatic contemporary events, seemingly casual, into an elaborate recapitulation of America's elevation of property over humanity. Between the Civil War and World War I the betrayal of freedom and the replacement of statesmen by magnates finalized the American Golden Rule still obeyed by the mayors of our cities in their "shoot to kill" proclamations. "The rights of property are more important than the right to life." [4]

2

Casualties marks the structural and thematic point of no return in *Tender Is the Night*. Henceforth, in *Escape* and *The Way Home*, Dick Diver is director without a cast, general without an army; he is man waiting, man pretending. Increasingly isolate, he drifts between a dying social and moral order of affection and illusion and "the whole new world in which he believed," an order formed by contingencies of circumstance and personality. If *Case History* anatomized the roots of psychic paralysis and *Rosemary's Angle* the gaping spaces among Diver's desires, critical perceptions, and life-style, *Casualties* fills out the historical context behind his disintegration.

To accomplish history, two decades of war and peace, linked morally and thematically, are rendered by Fitzgerald in two different modes—that of pathos and that of parody. As an event and as a cultural reference point World War I and the "broken universe" that followed indefinitely from it come to consciousness from Dick Diver's own broken heart. The tone, therefore, is Diver's mood of pathos. Fitzgerald's intention, however, is to demonstrate the lack of influence wrought by past history upon present and future conditions and values.

[4] A statement by Paul Elmer More, quoted by Claire Sachs, *The Seven Arts Critics* (Ph.D. dissertation, University of Wisconsin, 1955), p. 96.

He achieves this through parody. The contemporary dramatic events of *Casualties* elaborately and cynically repeat the history of the Civil War and Reconstruction. Throughout *Tender Is the Night* Diver and Grant, North and Lincoln, link Civil War and Reconstruction to World War I and "Normalcy," but in *Casualties* Fitzgerald replaces authorial allusion and reflection with structural parody. What we have in this middle book of the novel is the aesthetic application of Hegel's notion, reworked by Marx, that "all facts and personages of great importance in history occur, as it were, twice. He forgot to add: the first time as tragedy, the second as farce." [5]

Specifically, the moral imperatives of freedom and dignity, insofar as such causes were crucial to the Civil War, are rendered farcical in the dramatic climax of *Casualties*. Abe North (Lincoln as drunken cynic) falsely accuses "the prominent Negro restaurateur, Freeman" (168) of stealing a thousand francs, and calls the police. Freeman unjustly jailed, his friends murder Jules Peterson (J. P.), a black in complicity with North. The murder—exploitation of black by white—is callously dismissed by Diver who, like Grant on the historical stage, presides over his world's "reconstruction." Nicole, the violated body of America, when she unconsciously associates the blood (really Peterson's) on Rosemary's sheets (Dick and Rosemary, Devereux and Nicole) with her own violation, is told: " 'Look here, you mustn't get upset over this—it's only some nigger scrap' " (172). Diver's own subliminal violations do not allow him to tell Nicole that the rape of America and the murder and enslavement of black people are linked. He will not acknowledge, let alone bear, his share of the guilt. In any case his reassurance is the same one given to America in the crippling of the Freedmen's Bureau during the Grant administration, the same time when America was being reconstructed in the composite image

---

[5] Karl Marx, "The 18th Brumaire of Louis Bonaparte," *Basic Writings on Politics and Philosophy: Karl Marx and Friedrich Engel*, ed. Lewis S. Feuer (New York: Doubleday, 1959), p. 320.

of Robber Barons and Southern Bourbons. Victim Jules Peterson's occupation as manufacturer of shoe polish makes the parody complete. Recall Booker T. Washington's "Atlanta Compromise": "In all things that are purely social we can be as separate as the five fingers, and yet one as the hand in all things essential to mutual progress." [6] One year later *Plessy* v. *Ferguson* became the law of the land. Can it, then, come as any surprise that, in Fitzgerald's shrewdly racial analogy, "Abe's first hostile Indian (Freeman) had tracked the friendly Indian (Peterson) and . . . had hunted down and slain him" (172)? To whom other than W. E. B. DuBois should one go for assessment of the humanization process spelled out for black man and white man alike in this allegorical incident? "The history of the American Negro is the history of this strife,—this longing to attain self-conscious manhood, to merge to his double self into a better and truer self." [7] Divide and conquer or not, whatever the conscious and unconscious policies of annihilation, some men are indivisible—and free.

What is driven home hardest in *Casualties* is not only the worsening cycle of events but idealist Diver's failure to become an agent of change. There seemed a general need in the twenties, after the physical and psychic ravages of a war fought for illusions, to define history as Sancho Panza had defined fate centuries before: "a drunken, freakish drab, and blind into the bargain, so that she doesn't see what she's doing, nor does she know whom she raises nor whom she pulls down." [8] What safer way to banish guilt and justify exile than to deny any sense of moral or social purpose to the Civil War, or to any war? Consider Bill Gorton's typical comic outburst in Hemingway's *The Sun Also Rises*: "That was what the Civil War was about. Abraham Lincoln was a faggot. He was in love with General Grant. So

[6] Booker T. Washington, "The Atlanta Exposition Address," *Up from Slavery: An Autobiography* (New York: A. L. Burt, 1900), pp. 221–22.

[7] DuBois, *The Souls of Black Folk*, p. 17.

[8] Miguel de Cervantes Saavedra, *Don Quixote of La Mancha*, trans. and ed. by Walter Starkie (New York: New American Library, 1957), p. 416.

was Jefferson Davis. Lincoln freed the slaves on a bet. The Dred Scott case was framed by the Anti-Saloon League. Sex explains it all." [9] If one's balls were shot off for a lie in World War I, so must have been the case for the casualities of other noble wars. The tragedy is that the history of America from Civil War to World War I bears out the farce.

There is, in this generation's vision of history as parody, a fantasy of insulation, a calculated fantasy, seemingly of despair, but, in reality, an excuse for its reckless behavior. Against these utterly personal currents, the events and processes of history and the links among past, present, and future, among ancestors, himself, and descendants, always live intensely in Fitzgerald's imagination. This concern explains, better than any other reason, his decision to proceed from 1917, moment of mixed idealism and pragmatism (new empire rescues mother empire so that the American Revolution is, at last, forgiven), to 1930, time of crash for the American system and the emergence of God knows what new order of history. The "spring of 1917" heralded the zenith of bachelorhood for Dick Diver and seemingly for America. As idea and as force, America had yet to be legally wedded to the world empire; granted, there had been some casual pawings, but not yet total consummation.

What had not yet been resolved, either by Diver or by America, was the contrary pull toward absorption on the one hand and isolation on the other. If rootless, a blurred individuality creates uncertainty about where one's own being ends and others' begin. Fear of contact may then be generalized to abstraction. Sensuous, benevolent contact having failed Diver and his old America, the end of *Tender Is the Night* prophesies new forces to reconstruct the "broken universe of the war's ending." As Tommy Barban overpowers Nicole with his "eastern vision," the system openly identifies with the new pillage about to sweep the world. Yet will the system of America survive

[9] Ernest Hemingway, *The Sun Also Rises* (New York: Charles Scribner's Sons, 1926), p. 116.

the crash and the fascist coalitions springing from the rubble? Fitzgerald, it seems certain, thinks the answer is yes—yes, that is, if the marriage of dynastic heiress Warren and right-wing soldier Barban continues the metaphor of America and the forces which possess her.

3

Our introduction to *Casualties* is by way of Dick Diver's tour of Thiepval and Beaumont-Hamel—"tragic hill" and bloody battleground of World War I. He (and we, with one cold eye cast upon him) look backward at the war and try to grasp its historical-cultural significance as fatal demarcation line for Western civilization. Dick himself reflects on the holocaust's relation to the centuries since the Reformation. He does so not with disinterest or detachment but as an American male in the system—for Fitzgerald the given of the archetypal idealist is active engagement with the American social and economic system—as a man who will be torn apart and left without identity in a land, to him, bereft of any "spirit of place": " 'This western-front business couldn't be done again, not for a long time. The young men think they could do it but they couldn't. They could fight the first Marne again but not this. This took *religion* and *years of plenty* and *tremendous sureties* and the *exact relation* that existed *between the classes.*' " (118, my italics).

Religion—that moral, social, and personal world order in and beyond individuals or even generations—carried with its dogmas the notion of a community bound by a covenant greater than the sum of its believers, a covenant of mysterious and omniscient source.

Years of plenty—a prosperity rooted still in past and place— owed a tithe to the terrific economic base of empires which penalized backward (different) races and cultures into serfdom for the motherland or fatherland. There flourished together technology and empire, the nineteenth-century's verification in history of the Calvinist-Reformation doctrine of elected people and chosen nations.

Tremendous sureties—begin with the idea of election and damnation. Let history itself stage elections. Let the third world praise its own salvation in a separate heaven. Then "illusions of eternal strength and health, and of the essential goodness of people"—certain people and peoples—shall cease to seem illusions but become the objective nature of the world. Theology calls it the time of millennium.

Exact relation between the classes—everyone has a part to play in the imperial drama. Own the empire (upper classes), administer and service it (middle), or cheer its invincibility as proof of one's own national and racial superiority. Finally such cultures translate into a national chorus whose classes combine to celebrate religious truth and national legends and all the ensuing sureties, ideal and material, as history bears out these things.

Immediately, Diver further isolates the examples of western culture that he has in mind, examples whose connections to America's newest cycle of illusion (and power) and its coming realization in empire are unmistakable. In truth, he takes us back, spiritually and historically, to Lake Geneva or "the true center of the Western World": " 'The Russians and Italians weren't any good on this front. You had to have a *whole-souled sentimental equipment going back further than you could remember.* You had to remember Christmas, and postcards of the Crown Prince and his fiancée, and little cafés in Valence and beer gardens in Unter den Linden and weddings at the mairie, and going to the Derby, and your grandfather's whiskers' " (118, my italics). No fractured souls are among these bravely obedient. The Russians and Italians are excluded, it seems, because they were not culturally reshaped by that middle-class individual and national consciousness conceived during the Reformation. But Diver's snapshots are not of Calvinist doctrine or world view. What he photographs are the cultural consequences of the coalition between Protestantism and nationalism. No more pope meant no more authorities beyond national boundaries. Instead, power gravitated toward councils of bishops which councils mirrored developing national chambers or parliaments which, in turn, derived from councils of princes anxious to change the state metaphor from that of head (absolute power to the king) to that of *ship*. Diver's focus is also upon middle-class circumstances—Reformation, nationalism, and capitalism. Institutionalized, these elements established and propagated the middle classes. For middle-class memories, especially those of an increased stake and role in nineteenth-century government, culture, and empire, seduced English, Germans, and French into death in this tortuous military version of *Pilgrim's Progress*. Backwards and forwards, a foot at a time, the young men gave their lives to this ritual, a slow-motion dance orchestrated in brutal, mechanized assaults.

Finally, Diver's focus dissolves to love and war in these cultures:

> "Why this was a love battle—there was a century of middle-class love spent here. This was the last love battle."
> "You want to hand over this battle to D. H. Lawrence," said Abe.
> "All my beautiful lovely safe world blew itself up here with a great gust of high explosive love," Dick mourned persistently. "*Isn't that true, Rosemary?*" (118, my italics).

Diver's metaphor, comparing this battle's mass death to the universal consummation of a culture, suggests the diversion of erotic energy to war. That is to say, Diver's point of view, one that slogans like "Make the World Safe for Democracy" and "Protect Poor Little Belgium" upheld, visualizes a generation of Europeans going out to fight as if World War I were a crusade essential to the salvation of the Victorian order. Apparently, this generation (Diver certainly is among them; only

America's late involvement, one suspects, spared him its fate and allowed him his middle-class educational deferment) did not understand the other side of the nineteenth-century culture. Empires are not captured and held with clean hands, and the barbarian mechanical forest of weapons baptized in fratricidal blood during World War I exposed the murderous industrial will making real all those illusions nourished by the English, French, and German middle classes. Yet, if he is sad about the lives exploded to bits, Diver does not account for the process critically. His grief is wholly emotional; ultimately, he mourns for himself.

"I couldn't kid here," Diver wistfully tells Abe North who would stage, with pebbles, a mock artillery duel. "The silver cord is cut and the golden bowl is broken and all that, but an old romantic like me can't do anything about it" (118). The metaphor derives from Ecclesiastes where the prophet foretells the collapse of civilization; the cord of life's lamp is loosened until its golden bowl swings wildly, falls, and is broken on the ground. Diver, then, laments not so much the loss of his own youth and illusions as the severance of himself from Victorian culture and society. One can see Diver's particular sense of love expressed patriotically through illusions which end in war and death, and repeated by his own sublimation of desire into classic Victorian forms. Indeed Abe's allusion to Lawrence calls to mind that writer's vision of World War I as the fulfillment in history of the death urge by men with no other purpose in society, men whose marriages were sexually desolate. Consider as archetype of this, Egbert in "England, My England." Unwilling and unable to master his wife and family, economically or psychically, he becomes utterly dependent upon his wife's father, Godfrey Marshall. Though opposed to the war, Egbert, at the behest of Marshall, forsakes his family for the front and there dies for the abstractions of authority, nation, and empire, having been sent there by a very tangible master. Lawrence's viewpoint was shared in America by Randolph Bourne, who saw the war as a betrayal of America's needed domestic "Reconstruction": " 'In going to war, it [America] had itself been captured by the ancient tyrannies of the old world: nationalism, patriotism, militarism, state mysticism, formulas by means of which the human spirit had been held in an undeveloped, dependent, childish condition and in the bonds of an animal past.' " [10] Diver's own connection to this vicious framework of psychology and history paralyzes his being, for his nostalgic attachment to an illusory past prevents his intelligence from facing the horrors behind the facts of history, and, likewise, the facts of his life.

With Dick, however, the emergence of his desire for Rosemary will soon widen his schizophrenia. Work and responsibilities cannot much longer hold in formal, ordered place his long-submerged sexual impulses. As his European brothers had escaped and rallied to war because of incomplete social and sexual lives, Diver has confused work with love until his professional commitment dissolves into a parody of psychiatry. With Nicole, wife and patient, for partner, he "works over" eccentric personalities—"a French circus clown, Abe and Mary North, a pair of dancers, a writer, a painter, a comedienne from the Grand Guignol, a half-crazy pederast from the Russian Ballet, a promising tenor they had staked to a year in Milan" (149). He would, it must be said in his behalf, use Warren money to revitalize the arts, but perhaps at the expense of these artists facing up to themselves. One remembers, in this connection, Zelda Fitzgerald's compulsive, evasive, and tragic attempt to establish her ego through a dancing career. In his own life, Diver's substitution of nostalgia and sentimentality for historical and psychological intelligence is paralleled by his increasing attachment to Rosemary, who, unlike Nicole, is the perfect fantasy virgin.

In a moving passage, both tough and sympathetic, Fitzgerald

[10] Randolph Bourne, as quoted by Paul Rosenfeld, *Port of New York*, ed. Sherman Paul (Urbana: University of Illinois Press, 1961), p. 214.

shows Dick Diver's historical concern as short-lived, as, indeed, a weapon in the euphemistic arsenal of a genteel man on the make. "Then, leaving infinitesimal sections of Würtemburgers, Prussian Guards, Chasseurs Alpins, Manchester mill hands and Old Etonians to pursue their eternal dissolution under the warm rain, they took the train for Paris" (120). All classes are victims of this war, for its sustaining illusions had soaked into the soil of European national cultures. Diver, sentimental survivor of these dead, leads his troupe back to Paris and the therapeutic carnival, but these dead are still dead, still dissolving. Fitzgerald explicitly renders judgment upon Diver's tendency to make history pander to selfish emotion when he ends the chapter with Nicole reading "the guidebooks to the battlefield that Dick had brought along—indeed, he had made a quick study of the whole affair until it bore a faint resemblance to one of his own parties" (120). As in his relation to love, Dick's idealism creates for him a broken heart ("If life won't do it, it's not a substitute to get a broken heart") in place of war's broken body.

Back in life, Diver uses his power to evoke loss in order to gather his social unit more rigidly under his leadership. If one wants to talk about a pragmatic unconscious, then Diver's allegiance to a past whose tragedy lends itself to the sentimental and superficial brings Rosemary to full adulation of him. And she is exactly the daughter figure whom Victorian gentlemen would keep hands off, while secretly, pruriently, ravishing. So, complexly, Diver the director moves his cast, particularly the understudy female lead, further toward the point at which form and desire coincide. In addition, consciously, Diver eulogizes dead forms and generations to keep himself loyal to his own duty, which is directly to Nicole, and indirectly to the others— last of all, to Rosemary.

The unity of *Casualties* flows from the condition of individual, psychological casualty, inevitable for this centrifugal society's changing forms of creation and desire after the war's universal, Western casualty. Abe North, Monsieur Freeman, Maria

Wallis's anonymous Englishman, Jules Peterson, Nicole, and, finally, Dick Diver—these are the individual lives which veer toward violence and chaos. Like the events of World War I, there is both an accidental and a causal motion impelling these disintegrations. Abe North, for example, once a "brilliant and precocious" composer, now persuades himself of form's incapacity to hold together his disintegrating will to create and will to live. More and more he requires memory as a substitute for experience; to stir the memory alcohol is necessary, so his deterioration, internal and external, makes its journey along parallel rails.

Dramatically, in *Casualties*, Abe modulates "the lush moment outside time" to a darker and more prophetic key. His is a direction which, seeing only Dick's expertly directed reality, one cannot believe Diver will take. In Abe the facility and the burden of promise—early and easy success—combine with shallow roots, in music and in life, to bring about incapacitation. "All of them were conscious of the solemn dignity that flowed from him, of his achievement, fragmentary, suggestive, and surpassed" (145). As with Abe Lincoln, ugly circumstance will put a sudden end to his life. But, unlike Lincoln, Abe had already handed down his own sentence. When Nicole tries to fix Abe's tragedy in the present tense of particularly American dissipation, Dick hints that creation and destruction are poles of the same temperament and energy—"smart men play close to the line because they have to—some of them can't stand it, so they quit" (161). But the real action of *Casualties* dissects the nature of this psychological-aesthetic margin in Dick Diver himself. The continuing reference point is his relationship with Rosemary which gradually ceases to be a scenario written, directed, and produced by Diver.

4

Love as role and role as love—*Daddy's Girl* changes the nature of the drama. This is Rosemary's show; Diver and the others now watch her in a movie that spells out the preoccupations of American culture with Rosemary's talent debased by the values it serves. "There she was—embodying all the immaturity of the race, cutting a new cardboard paper doll to pass before its empty harlot's mind" (130). The technology of celluoid further distills youth into sentimentality and superficiality. Heroine begins as fetching little girl and changes (reversing the romance mode) into a cardboard doll whose very one-dimensional youth and aggressive immaturity give her parental status over the race which is audience. Her mind appears empty and cheap, open to and accustomed to corruption—the corruption, however, of the self-deceived: "Before her tiny fist the forces of lust and corruption rolled away; nay, the very march of destiny stopped, inevitably became evitable; syllogism, dialectic, all rationality fell away" (130). All for love of Rosemary, and, on her part, all for love of Daddy.

Thus Hollywood vision parodies Emerson's idealism. The eye creates the world, but in this case the eye's medium is celluloid, a substance created by the mind and molded to serve the profit system. *Daddy's Girl* charges an incestuous price for its assurances of innocence. For after it rolls away outward corruption, there remain in Eden no Adams but only God and Eve, father and daughter, "united at the last in a father complex so apparent that Dick winced for all psychologists at the vicious sentimentality" (131). The obsession with rooting out an external condition of evil gets its moral authority from an ingrown, incestuous relationship. Ultimately, the movie implies, Rosemary triumphs not because of any strength or independence, but because she is daddy's girl. One thinks of Orphan Annie and Daddy Warbucks. In both contexts innocence means opposition to experience unless that experience confirms existing illusions, i.e., the divine quality of Daddy's fortune, empire, and vision.

But truest to the daughter archetype in *Tender Is the Night* may be Fitzgerald's assertion that the will of daddy's little girl halts or even annihilates historical process, that, because of her will, "syllogism, dialectic, all rationality fell away" (130). Perhaps the overall male-female context that Fitzgerald alludes to will be clearer if we consider his assertion after Baby Warren successfully intimidates the American Consul in Rome: "The American Woman, aroused, stood over him; the clean-sweeping irrational temper that had broken the moral back of a race and made a nursery out of a continent, was too much for him" (251). Men occupy the nursery. At the other end of the father-daughter complex is the reduction of men to impotence, to moral children lacking will and purpose. One remembers Fitzgerald's allusion to frontier mothers who denied the existence of wolves and thus created in their children a massive structure of psychological and historical illusion. What, one wonders, were their men doing? Or were many of them dead from attempts to conquer the land, to subdue and exterminate its natives? Did male energy, occupied with survival and domination beyond the wife and family, create through its very absence, its imposition on women of a dual role, the American woman as aroused, insatiable, and, finally, destructive male? Twisted, Adam's image of Eve has come back to destroy its creator.

Is it any wonder, given these sexual annihilations and given the factual horrors of World War I, that "all America after the war turned to *Little Women*"? Why? Waldo Frank went on persuasively to answer his own question. "Was it not because the only meaning of [men's] life had been in childhood? Maturity had nothing to offer them: it was only before they had started to make a living that they had lived. Boyhood meant home: maturity meant, not a larger home, but exile." [11] Weak

11 Waldo Frank, *The New America* (New York: Boni-Liveright, 1922), p. 162.

or absent fathers change their wives into men who in turn mother their sons until these shrink in manhood from the demands of other women. From such threads do men weave tapestries upon which wife and daughter are one and the same figure. If we consider America not simply as woman but as daughter, does not the self-righteous outrage expressed by its masters when their schemes are opposed become more comprehensible? Need I cite the example of Lyndon Johnson on Vietnam and student protestors—young men wooing an America regarded by her masters as their property, indeed as their private aesthetic creation? Was not guilt involved in the President's almost personal escalation of aggressive violence? Protestors possessing America as woman would be bad enough, but America as daughter? And black protestors!

In the immediate context of *Tender Is the Night*, Diver, the symbolic father, perceives the implications of neurosis and incest fantasy. But he perceives those things out there. On the celluloid, in the culture. He does not see, even after their rehearsal of an explicitly sexual and implicitly incestuous scene, his relationship with Rosemary as an illustration of the father complex. His complicity in the fantasy is particularly horrifying because, as psychiatrist, he should recognize his fantasies and the shattering effect they, if merely sensed, would have on Nicole. In the second place he is repeating the transformation of a particular woman into ideal image. Perplexed about his own past and present, he seeks in Rosemary the innocence of body and psyche which Devereux's violation seems to have denied him with Nicole. Psychiatrist is now paternal sexual initiator, so that he can refresh and re-create his vision of youth and beauty and make image flesh in Rosemary. She, having had no lasting father and only celluloid lovers, unites protector and violator in the same man. For her part, she seeks the very situation responsible for Nicole's schizophrenia. Thus, with not even an inner hunch about the disintegrative complexities involved, Rosemary pursues the affair with a naive willfulness worthy of her persona in *Daddy's Girl*. Increasingly Dick goes along, his practical objections nullified by his pull toward the fountain of youth, the double initiation ritual. He does not yet know that the wake of his fantasy will pull him closer and closer to the isles of forgetfulness and, ultimately, toward loss of the mind which set ideal sail in the first place.

To get back to the film and the cultural viewpoint it defines —there is a way in which *Daddy's Girl* legitimizes to Diver his desire for Rosemary. For although the film cannot be, because of its crudeness, a conscious reference point for his values, Diver, in his gentleman's guise, is taken by the affection and the motive behind Rosemary's offer of a screen test for him—"so you'd come out and be my leading man in a picture" (131). Of course, he chooses to ignore the complication that they would remake *Daddy's Girl* in a more genteel mode: "He was overwhelmed. 'It was a *darn sweet* thought, but I'd rather look at *you*. You were *about the nicest* sight I ever looked at'" (131, except for *you*, my italics). So Rosemary's trump card works superbly after all. Since she included him in her outside world, Diver, who is afloat, personally and professionally, yields to her. Indeed, he capitulates in the desperate, gawky language of a Eugene O'Neill farmboy, or, in *Tender Is the Night*, of nitwit, Collis Clay. What has just been peremptorily rejected by Diver in terms of the movies—being Rosemary's "leading man"—is now true in life. Suddenly he must have her, and, actors together, they conspire in passwords to free themselves of Collis Clay's "offensive bulk of the third party" (132). By short strokes, the film fantasy has become the most urgent reality of their experience. And who knows what has been transpiring in and beyond the movie palaces across America?

Resolved in their intimacy, they arrive at an abrupt, staccato social world expressed through the changed structure of what had been "the frame of Cardinal de Retz' palace" (133). In a different way this scene verifies the vision of personality as actor, experience as drama, the world as set—in short, the principle of contingency, the relative principle. The still evolving, contingent reality presented here through the materials and forms of architecture foreshadows the mode of perception which captures the novel in its final stages.

The eighteenth-century futurist architecture of the house —masonry to steel and glass—recapitulates the evolution of consciousness from past to future, with the present still a vague and unfulfilled state. Spatial present is nonexistent; carbon has changed to diamond without any process of becoming. Likewise, temporally, no present exists. Life as exhibition has become life on a directorless set. As personalities, the guests cease to exist; they are objects manipulated in a futurist dream architecturally realized: "The outer shell, the masonry, seemed rather to enclose the future, so that it was an electric-like shock, a definite nervous experience, perverted as a breakfast of oatmeal and hashish, to cross that threshold, if it could be so called, into the long hall of blue steel, silver gilt, and the myriad facets of many oddly bevelled mirrors" (133). This is a world of mere angles and relative fields so that each step, each glance, changes all that one sees and all of oneself seen by anyone else. No longer are Diver and Rosemary as they were at the Decorative Arts Exhibition—spectators observing future forms from a fixed point in the present. In this context no such reference point exists. "No one knew what this room meant because it was evolving into something else, becoming everything a room was not; to exist in it was as difficult as walking on a highly polished moving stairway" (133). Not only is the ground moving away from one's feet in conflicting and shifting centrifugal-centripetal patterns, but the world of objects beyond oneself is changing continually in shape, size, and density. Finally, an individual— in this setting the very concept is anachronistic—absolutely has no control over his perceptions or perceptual field and no choice about how he perceives.

Rosemary, for instance, "had the detached false-and-exalted feeling of being on a set," but this experience differs from her relationship to movie set as the star for whom the synthetic world has been created. In this scene there is imagined and realized a new mode of consciousness and personality, one as different from the essentialist vision as steel and glass are from masonry in architectural construction. Environment both reflects and creates a human sensibility which is metallic, barbed, and utterly without depth or density; in short, the environment has become a monster.

At first, Rosemary cannot operate in this reality of surfaces, a world in which nuance and technique provide the only meaning, a sliding reality. Indeed, she barely can sustain the mere imitations of a bit player; her personality appears nonfunctional unless there is present a director to create a world and guide her through it. What gets her through is no new sense either of herself or of other objects but her training in mechanical, automatic response; so she moves about the room "in a series of semi-military turns, shifts, and marches" (134). Insincerely, automatically, her attention rivets on the boyish girl who ravishes her in indirect, lesbian fashion, but her other, curious self is compelled by three women, compared to mannequins and cobras, who are wooden and venomous, and who anatomize the Divers and North with surgical precision—autopsy form. Finally, leaving this world and its "corrugated surfaces" of perception, language, and personality, Diver and Rosemary seize upon each other as a means of stabilizing reality. In a world of criticism, uncertainty, hostility, and increasing chaos, Diver cannot not respond to Rosemary's extravagant admiration. His self-indulgence represents no foray into the future, into a relationship on different terms from his marriage, but is instead a re-enactment of his child-wife situation with Nicole. But where, given the mode of repetition, is his critical faculty, his moral faculty; above all, where are his self-awareness and his sense of form?

5

Henceforth to the violent denouement of *Casualties*, deterioration stands as fact, no longer probability. Abe North is the first to crack. Grotesquely, his individual chaos spreads out from him in the form of disrupted lives and, finally, murder. But for Dick Diver disintegration goes on within, almost invisibly. Horribly for everyone concerned, his affair with Rosemary derives its nourishment from the mask of propriety worn by the lovers.

For Diver has grown to manhood formed by genteel illusions —"nothing could be superior to the 'good instincts,' honor, courtesy, and courage" (221)—illusions displaced from Victorian England to America so that the middle class, particularly, could dissociate itself from the horrors of aggression and rape on the American continent, just as gentility had seemed to disconnect the English from exploitation in Africa (Diver is a Rhodes scholar) and Asia. Thus Diver's euphemistic vision of nineteenth-century culture allows him to sentimentalize World War I as the end of an epoch in which these, in fact mythical, "good instincts" were realized. North's melancholy and despair, though equally real, are uncoded. His hopelessness derives more from a universal "sense that life is essentially a cheat and its conditions those of defeat" than from any particular analysis of history and culture.[12] Yet even this despair at the truth of defeat and death in human life comes from an early idealism whose purity and intensity are peculiarly American, the character of which Fitzgerald spelled out to his daughter in 1940 as the world raged in holocaust. "You speak of how good your generation is, but I think they share with every generation since the Civil War in America the sense of being somehow about to in-

[12] Andrew Turnbull, ed., *The Letters of F. Scott Fitzgerald* (New York: Charles Scribner's Sons, 1963), p. 96.

herit the earth." [13] Through a dispensation of myth and magic those who succeed to America imagine they escape that psychic inheritance tax demanded by their national past.

Dramatically, the immediate violence by Maria Wallis against her Englishman shatters whatever calm Diver had commanded for Nicole and Rosemary. As war had been seen through the language of love, so love is told through the metaphor of war. This time the shrapnel allusion finds Dick on its receiving end, for, unlike his elegy on Thiepval, he can make no "moral comment." In addition to this discord of physical and psychic "concussions," Fitzgerald modulates from the "lush mid-summer moment outside time" (175) to the stench of a "suspended mass of gasoline exhaust" from which there was "no promise of rural escape," "only roads choked with the same foul asthma" (148). Increasingly, their carnival environment assumes a sterile, claustrophobic, stifling quality—the atmosphere of landscape after a battle.

The beasts of repression loosening, Diver can contain no longer his desire for Rosemary and the fear that he will not possess her *first*, and so the detachment which made him unique is menaced: "Dignified in his fine clothes, with their fine accessories, he was yet swayed and driven as an animal. Dignity could come only with an overthrowing of his past, of the effort of the last six years" (152–53). Beneath the elegant form and genteel dignity of his clothes lives the male, his sexual desires beating against the creases of his social training. "Dignity" refers to Diver's essential value as a man, a male who confronts the simple as well as the complex demands of his being. Yet Diver's choice of Rosemary Hoyt brings out into the open the conflict at the root of his schizophrenia. For of all women in the world, Rosemary Hoyt is the one least capable of liberating him from a marriage in which his sexuality, purpose, and manhood serve in opposition to his basic desire. To use a colonial analogy, it is as

[13] *Ibid.*

if Diver's personality (Uncle Tom) subverts his manhood (Bigger Thomas). Like Nicole of six years ago, Rosemary wants no dominant male, no turmoil, no chaos, no violence, of whatever kind. "Rosemary saw him always as a model of correctness" (153). So if Diver wants Rosemary, he'd better stick to the genteel mode—male wolf better conceal himself in the fatherly shepherd's clothing. But, at the same time, if he keeps to the genteel way, there will be no "overthrowing of his past," no essential dignity. In this situation, then, fulfillment cannot happen directly, man to woman and male to female, simultaneously. Sexuality, when indulged in, must be called something else than the personal exigency it is.

Fitzgerald's analytic reflection—"Dick's necessity of behaving as he did was a projection of some submerged reality" (153)—has its antecedent in Diver's earlier sexual skirmishes with "only hot-cheeked girls in hot secret rooms." Henceforth, sexual energy had gone into work. Now we see a split in Diver between sexuality and personality. Perhaps if Rosemary were not a personality to him, and a dependent one confirming his fantasy of Adam and the rib, he could take her without all the feelings of guilt.

After he describes Diver's coat sleeve, shirt sleeve, and wrist as so many fixed circles—clothes as prophylactic casings for the body—Fitzgerald concludes the anatomy of this divided self: "He was compelled to walk there or stand there . . . just as another man once found it necessary to stand in front of a church in Ferrara [Canossa], in sackcloth and ashes. Dick was paying some tribute to things unforgotten, unshriven, unexpurgated" (153). Henry IV went to Canossa in 1077 to ask Pope Gregory's forgiveness and absolution over the matter of lay investiture; the fate of his kingdom and of himself required the humiliation. Not so with Diver. Diver's pilgrimage pays tribute to desires first repressed then glossed over in the elegance and gentility of his life-style. Unconfessed, his sexual desires cannot be expurgated from the book of his life. The horror is that Diver seeks redress at a sacrilegious shrine. Rosemary cannot exorcise his demons, only arouse them and chase them into deeper hiding in his heart. So, with each revolution, the repressive cycle swings a narrower arc. If Diver's sexual focus upon Nicole was tragic, that same impulse fixed six years later on a Rosemary Hoyt seems like farce. Even Dick perceives this, aesthetically, and is terrified by the persistence of his obsession: "Back at two o'clock in the Roi George corridor the beauty of Nicole had been to the beauty of Rosemary as the beauty of Leonardo's girl was to that of the girl of an illustrator. Dick moved on through the rain, demoniac and frightened, the passions of many men inside him and nothing simple that he could see" (166). America, too, with Rosemary as its cultural embodiment, has grown farcical, its newest fantasies of innocence all wrapped in celluloid for the infantile mind.

Through contemporary experience history does intervene. Abe North's whimsical interference with the black community in Paris victimizes Monsieur Freeman and causes the murder of the sycophantic Peterson. When the distress call comes from Freeman's friends, Diver is playing sexual anagrams with Rosemary. And Nicole, given a chance to exhibit some of the human sympathy she expects from the world—"'He says there is a Meestaire Freeman into prison that is a friend of the whole world'" (158)—disdains the "injustice" with a "vehement clap of the receiver," and goes off on another spree of wholesale buying.

But what, for Fitzgerald, is the moral relationship between history and parody, injustice and self-indulgence? Is it really farfetched to claim that through irony and parody he censures the degradation of the black people in his society? Consider the tough racial judgment arrived at during his attempt to reconstruct his own personality: "And just as the laughing stoicism which has enabled the American Negro to endure *the intolerable conditions of his existence* has cost him his sense of the truth—

so in my case there is a price to pay." [14] Written in 1936, the above may clarify a fascinating parallel between Scott Fitzgerald and Richard Wright in their relationship to the Communist party:

> I have become disgusted with the party leadership and have only health enough left for my literary work, so I'm on the sidelines. It had become a strain making speeches at "Leagues Against Imperialistic War," *and their treatment of the Negro question.. finished me.*[15]

> [Richard] was certain that the Party would not approve of *an honest portrayal of Negroes*—they had to be heroes, not human beings.[16]

Finally, the aesthetics of personality—human integrity and diversity—unite black and white novelist in a bond stronger than ideology. So long as the Communist (or any other) party would manipulate, distort, and therefore debase personality for its own ends, each of these men would choose artistic morality over Machiavellian politics. In the case of Fitzgerald, the truth of black-white relations, as parodied in *Tender Is the Night*, took precedence over the commitment to the Communist world ideology so prevalent and so fashionable for his generation in the thirties.[17]

[14] Fitzgerald, *The Crack-Up*, ed. Edmund Wilson (New York: New Directions, 1945), p. 84. My italics.

[15] Turnbull, ed., *Letters of F. Scott Fitzgerald*, p. 417. My italics.

[16] Constance Webb, *Richard Wright: A Biography* (New York: G. P. Putnam's Sons, 1968), p. 135. My italics.

[17] Two issues cross here: Fitzgerald's attitude toward race and the Communist party's use of the Scottsboro boys. On the first, there can be no doubt that Fitzgerald drastically changed his views. In a May, 1921, letter to Edmund Wilson, for example, he writes such things as "the negroid streak creeps northward to defile the Nordic race," and "already the Italians have the souls of blackamoors." Four years later he ridicules these same views through Tom Buchanan in *The Great Gatsby*. By the end of his life he is writing intensely sympathetic sketches about black persons, i.e., "Dearly Beloved," written in the late thirties and published for the first time in the *Fitzgerald/Hemingway Annual* 1969. In addition Fitzgerald makes the black man whom Stahr and Kathleen meet on a beach a voice of moral taste in *The Last Tycoon*. About the Communist party and the Scottsboro case Fitzgerald was not alone in question-

In the different case of Dick Diver, sentimentally vicious perception about American history coincides with his own ongoing history as he responds to the presence of American war widows—gold stars given for their dead men—with visions of Confederate glory in the Civil War: "For a while the sobered women who had come to mourn for their dead, for something they could not repair, made the room beautiful. Momentarily, he sat again on his father's knee, riding with Mosby while the old loyalties and devotions fought on around him" (162). At the risk of placing ideology above integrity, I will say that I identify the Mosby allusion less with lost courage than with its lost romantic cause. For Diver's reverie into an old memory illustrates a polarity between courage and decadence, manners and false morality—in short, Diver's lack of a coherent, humanely inclusive historical context. To invert Yeats's "Second Coming": "passionate intensity" exists split off from any dynamic vision of history. Men of courage neglected the creation of a moral base of action.

Historically, then, as well as psychologically, Diver is attracted to virginity-violation archetypes. "Old loyalties and devotions"? " 'Good instincts'—honor, courtesy, and courage." These ideals mean one thing in the *legend* of chivalry and another in the *history* of America, particularly that of the South. Slavery and aristocracy; toil and leisure; white virgins worshipped, black woman raped. In repetition of his personal fantasies and desires, Diver superimposes chivalric legend upon gruesome history. It does seem to suit his isolation, his uneasy sense of himself as the last romantic, this identification with causes and events

---

ing the party's integrity. W. E. B. DuBois in *Dusk of Dawn* (pp. 297–99) accused the party of putting ideology above the fate of the young black men involved. "Had it not been for their senseless interference, these poor victims of Southern injustice would today be free. . . . But in the case of the Communists the actual fate of these victims was a minor matter. . . . Right as they undoubtedly were on the merits of the case, they were tragically wrong in their methods if they were seeking to free these victims." Look at *Native Son* and *Invisible Man* for fictional treatment of the Communist party's refusal to deal honestly with the race and personality of individual black men.

which put an end not only to courageous men, but to the societies and cultures behind them—except that the Civil War led to Reconstruction's alliance between Northern tycoons and Southern leisure gentlemen. (Or is this metaphorically the alliance fancied by Diver as a solution to his dilemma of society and self?) But in neither past nor present, history or novel, will the center of Diver's vision hold. For, in *Tender Is the Night* as in history, the Freemans are jailed by the vicious self-indulgence of the Norths—the cynically reconstructed union.

Form continues to incriminate desire. Indeed, Diver's desires for Rosemary are much less maddening than the jealously possessive father-daughter mode chosen to express them: "Almost with an effort he turned back to his two women at the table and faced the whole new world in which he believed. —Do you mind if I pull down the curtain?" (162). Any maturity of perception—renunciation of the corrupt "romantic" Confederate lost cause, for example—which might accrue to Diver's acceptance of "the whole new world" is drowned out by the refrain. Curtains conceal. Although Diver's sexual curiosity is prurient (how far did that college boy go with my Rosemary in the closed compartment?), metaphorically he draws a curtain between self-awareness and the reality of his own story and history. The nightmare remains, but like its legendary cultural counterpart, it remains unaccounted for. It is for us to reconstruct the ongoing nightmare, historically, rationally, factually.

Despite the roosting chickens of guilt, the climactic encounter in life might well be a scene from that ideal movie into which Rosemary has projected herself and Dick:

> When she opened the door she saw him as something fixed and godlike as he had always been, as older people are to younger, rigid and unmalleable.

· · · ·

> "Miss Television," he said with a lightness he did not feel. He put his gloves, his brief-case on the dressing table, his stick

against the wall. His chin dominated the lines of pain around his mouth, forcing them up into his forehead and the corner of his eyes, like fear that cannot be shown in public.

"Come and sit on my lap close to me," he said softly, "and let me see about your lovely mouth" (167).

Language and gesture conceal the inner chaos. But Abe North's reappearance and the murder of Jules Peterson abruptly halt their ambiguous interlude. In this situation, Diver at last changes allegiance from Nicole to Rosemary. All his charm, all his powers of ingratiation, serve the salvation of Rosemary's reputation and career. Recall the scandal of Fatty (Rosco Conkling) Arbuckle and Virginia Rappe in 1921. Sexual foul play between fat man and beautiful young woman might pale before revelations of Diver ("middle-aged gent," as he calls himself), Rosemary (the original, virginal Daddy's Girl), and a black man murdered on her bed. Though there has been victimization, THERE MUST BE NO SCANDAL. It is better, Diver's choice implies, to set off a new breakdown within Nicole than to tarnish Rosemary's national image, vicious as it is, of innocence.

Consider Diver's simple act—handing Nicole the bloody coverlet from Rosemary's bed and giving Rosemary the spread from Nicole's bed—and its complex effect on Nicole: "Nicole knelt beside the tub swaying sidewise and sidewise. 'It's you!' she cried, '—it's you come to intrude on the only privacy I have in the world—with your spread with red blood on it. I'll wear it for you—I'm not ashamed, though it was such a pity. On All Fools Day we had a party on the Zurichsee, and all the fools were there, and I wanted to come dressed in a spread but they wouldn't let me—'" (174). The symbolic recurrence— in fact this time a black man who would not be humanized by free blacks is murdered by them—is clear. Diver and Rosemary present Nicole with a bloody sheet, for disposal, which triggers not only her memory of paternal violation, but also the sense that she, already violated, not forcefully but through her father's hypocritical use of the protective illusion, is now involved with Diver (Bluebeard) as an accessory to his violation of Rosemary. And Nicole's paranoia does have roots in reality. Diver and Rosemary were sexually engaged when interrupted by North and Peterson. In terms of Diver's archetypal character, we see here a spontaneous tendency to throw all his weight behind preservation of the latest model of American innocence and intactness.

And Rosemary, the one saved? Her response to the mystery of the Villa Diana? "She answered the phone and almost cried with relief when she found it was Collis Clay" (174). She chooses illusion, the illusion of innocence manufactured in her upbringing and movie career, over the realities of violation, madness, and general human pain. The world of human pain, no matter, she will be Daddy's Girl—"Ooo-ooo-tweet, de tweetest thing, wasn't she dest too tweet?" (130). For Nicole's obsessive and fragmented viewpoint, there is now much to be said. Chaos, it seems, will out and render whatever psychological order one imposes absurd as an April Fool's Day trick. At this point, her own and the general history notwithstanding, Nicole's notion of personality as the sum of immediate contexts seems to have been vindicated. History cannot be ordered until its facts are collected and understood.

The twin coda to *Casualties* consists of Diver's farewell interview with Mrs. Speers and his resumption of domesticity with Nicole. From Rosemary's mother Dick is shocked to learn that she gave the go-ahead to her daughter, generally, because "women are necessarily capable of almost anything [frontier mothers again] in their struggle for survival" (176), and specifically, because she did not think Rosemary capable of being damaged by an affair with Dick. Thus Mrs. Speers and Baby Warren— the one favorably disposed toward Diver, the other unfavorably—view him identically. Whatever may be his own fascination with guilt, violation, and disintegration, the fact is that he cannot hurt either Rosemary or Nicole in any final way. The South will not rise again; and why should it—its policies, if not its structures, have been internalized by the nation itself.

Mind and desire, work and love, and the increasingly torturous relationship between these things, define the new regimen for Dick and Nicole. Diver's massive confidence about his writing has ebbed to the point where he thinks of retrenchment. "He had about decided to brief the work in its present condition and publish it in an undocumented volume of a hundred thousand words as an introduction to more scholarly volumes to follow" (178). If the circumference of his creative mind has narrowed, the aftermath of Paris signals a similar contraction of Dick as social personality. His psychiatrist's depth of field has been more and more squeezed into a family closeup. For order and for sanity's sake he must "banish the ghost of Rosemary before it became walled up with them" (180). But the suffering heart needs Rosemary's image, so Dick must act, a mode of pretense Nicole sees through enough to realize that their journey home is for the first time a "going away rather than a going toward" (179).

Casualties concludes with Diver's reflections on his state of captivity. For this stag the Warren estate has become a deer park off limits to all but one deer. All that Diver's asceticism has accomplished has been an insufficient "qualified financial independence" (183); he has mastered nothing and created nothing, neither as psychiatrist nor as husband and father. Once an agent of destiny, Diver has become himself a small business "constantly inundated by a trickling of goods and money" (183). The consciousness which had once seemed impervious to time past and in command of time present and future, that had seemed invulnerable before history, is now trapped in immobility. Previously, the hope and experience, then the drama, of Dick Diver's life seemed to suspend time and all of its destroying processes; time had seemed a creation of mind subject to imagination's hypnotic powers. But now the idealist is in bondage

to time, the living casualty of a historical motion and devasta-
tion which he has failed to apply to himself. As much as any
of those war dead whom he mourned, Dick Diver is a casualty
of those illusions of heroic service and national goodness under
whose flag he and millions of young men served a system of
class and empire whose dynamic was destructive of anyone who
idealized it with his unquestioning "whole-souled sentimental
equipment." Though his illusions dissipate, Diver's commitment
to the false old continuities paralyzes him; he can neither
abandon his household nor can he change its direction. So "he
stayed in the big room listening to the buzz of the electric
clock, listening to time" (183). Aware of time's impersonal
power, yet he must respond like a dumb man—the prisoner of
an empire more actual than his illusions and stronger than his
personality.

Casualties, which began with Diver as moral and historical
authority, as the personality who persuaded his women "that
there were no wolves [unknown forces, chaotic forces; forces of
darkness] outside the cabin door," ends with Diver as an auditor
who listens to time, but listens with a detachment tinged with
impotence and terror. Hopelessly paralyzed as a man, he cannot qualify, articulate, or interpret either time's meaning or his
own relation to it. Plagued no longer by the nightingale, but
only by the "buzz of the electric clock," Dick Diver will continue
to live a casualty of the old forms and illusions as they reappear
in the sentimental songs of his own time:

> "Just picture you upon my knee
> With tea for two and two for tea
> And me for you and you for me—" (183).

seven

Escape: We are all guilty, but guilty of what?

1

Throughout *Escape*, Dick Diver, like the Western democracies of the period, faces his life's moment of truth. Having perceived the fact and extent of his own and his culture's casualties, Diver has arrived at a Cartesian crisis. The Victorian romantic's "I believe, therefore I am" has yielded to the modern skeptic's "I doubt, therefore I am." This latter perception can lead to a blank reality, "a new world, material without being real" (123), as in *The Great Gatsby*, or it can "move man into a reality that he creates through reason rather than the one he has inherited and lived in." [1] Diver, however—his response may parallel that of the West to its past and to emerging totalitarian forms—does not see the moral and historical corollary to the Cartesian assertion. He does not see that "everything is possible not only in the *realm* of *ideas* but in the *field* of *reality* itself." [2]

The truth is that history can take any hypothesis and act on it. Obviously, this notion works in ways both fulfilling and despoiling. Fitzgerald's life, with its mid-thirties crack-up and late-thirties reintegration, seems to mirror the West's psychic history; in 1936 he looked back fifteen years to when the world itself,

[1] Neil Kleinman, *The Shape of Ideas and the Form of Art* (Ph.D. dissertation, University of Connecticut, 1965), p. ix.
[2] *Ibid.*, p. vii.

the terrible chimera of American success, appeared to realize every dream projected by the self. "This philosophy fitted on to my early adult life, when I saw the improbable, the implausible, often the 'impossible,' come true." [3] But the self as superman evolves—only with great effort after total collapse—into the self as "cracked plate," which "will not be brought out for company, but will do to hold crackers late at night or to go into the icebox under left-overs. . . ." [4] History too will go from dream—peace, prosperity, and justice—to nightmare—manic wars, world depression, purges, and death camps. The point is that, for Diver and for the culture he is emblem of, history, if not humanized, will brutalize humanity. Not Diver, not anyone, can escape. If he remains suspended in doubt, then history, whose motion of forces itself will carry on the creation of reality, will blow him off the transcendental masthead. Neither will its winds be gentle, as Diver discovers in Mussolini's Rome. Finally, Diver, escapist from self and from history, is stalked by an increasingly brutal civilization whose hounds will not be put off the scent by his journeys farther and farther away from the twentieth century.

Escape carries to climax the journey metaphor, invoked on many fronts, at the end of *Casualties*. Externally and internally, Diver experiences demonic release. This is not the dynamic release of exorcism where dammed-up energies are released pell-mell so that then the personality can express itself in new contacts with others and with the world. No, Diver's deliverance is from restriction and repression into a freedom that is not freedom but only violence, which, though it shreds his mask, his persona of the "good instincts," leaves him fragments of self which he cannot arrange because of paralyzing doubt. Indeed the Humpty-Dumpty allusion Diver directs at Baby Warren illuminates the shattering of his own soul: "It would be hundreds of years

[3] F. Scott Fitzgerald, *The Crack-Up*, ed. Edmund Wilson (New York: New Directions, 1945), p. 69.
[4] *Ibid.*, p. 75.

before any emergent Amazons would ever grasp the fact that a man is vulnerable only in his pride, but delicate as Humpty Dumpty once that is meddled with" (193). But this delicacy invoked by Diver is exactly the factor destructive of Humpty. All the king's horses and all the king's men, and presumably the king himself, are alive and well; only Humpty, the court fool, is dismembered, fragmented, and destroyed. So will it be with Diver, who, unlike Humpty's ghost, will not have the consolation that the mighty are working to reconstruct him. For *Escape* is about the attempt to refound self and order upon rotted beams, and about the volcanic upheaval of self and relationship, an upheaval which, in its transference of focus and energy, consumes, consumes, consumes.

Space and time: place after place becomes illusory refuge from time's onrush and from the paralysis of Diver's creative faculties, psychiatric and sexual. Personality and psychiatry: wife and patients reverse themselves. For Nicole, Diver restates the universe, but her attraction as a woman recedes. He lies to an afflicted artist about the complexity of consciousness, but as a man goes out to her "unreservedly, almost sexually" (201). Like America, Diver's resources are exhaustible. Like the earth in Christ's metaphor, both are losing savor without gaining compensatory vitality.

2

There is, in *Escape*, an acute consciousness of the paradoxical relation between man and time. For the mind can move in a linear way; it is not necessarily the prisoner of cyclic recurrence. Man sees spring and winter, day and night, life and death, all coming to pass again and again in the cosmos, yet he knows he must live and die once, a vanishing spot on time's horizon. More and more obsessively, Dick Diver flees life's particularities and continuities to search for his lost self in persons and places still to be created by his idealizing imagination. More and more he is reduced to mind and eye; these faculties, in turn, have grown more and more self-contained and set off from other realities, even from the rest of Diver's body.

Consider his elegaic response to a winter's interlude at Gstaad: "Good-bye, Gstaad! Good-bye, fresh faces, cold sweet flowers, flakes in the darkness. Good-bye, Gstaad, good-bye!" (195). Rhythm and refrain call to mind the Ophelia reference that recurs in *Tender Is the Night*. Diver associates Gstaad, its beauty, gaiety, and, above all, its distance from the course of his life, with individual and historical interludes of innocence— an innocence made precious by the tragedy of violation. As in *Hamlet*, innocence and promise are ground up in a context of power, in which the demands of survival dissolve personality into centrifugal dramatic roles. Yet the differences indict Dick Diver. Ophelia's "good night, sweet ladies," touches observers because in madness, powerlessness, and isolation, she can do nothing but create "sweet ladies" to receive her flowers. Diver, however, is not mad, but simply unable to confront his context or the sources of power that enforce it. In any case he too goes to images divorced from any continuing context, images like those flashing at one's face from the darkness on a train journey. But judgment must be rendered upon Diver's disconnected images, if only to recall that Fitzgerald has displayed a Gstaad in which facts—of wealth, power, and impotence—subordinate images. He has shown how Diver's thoughts and desires have come more and more absolutely to reside within himself with only occasional points of reference sliding into outside reality.

Although the Divers live at their clinic for almost four years, this condenses to the pattern of one day as we follow Diver on his grounds of the hopeless personalities, hopeless largely because of their "ceaseless round of ratiocination" (198). Such a perceptual sequence fixes objects and experiences, ignores fluctuations of extension, of time and space, and does not, cannot, confront realities one by one "in a line as with normal people but in the same circle. Round, round, and round. Around forever" (198). This describes a recurrent, repetitive, finally mythic way of seeing oneself and the world. What Fitzgerald makes us see, indirectly, is Diver's own abandoment, when it comes to his buried desires and needs, of a rationalist and historical way of being. Automatic returns to the past carry with them the assumption that circumstances and persons are not unique but correspond to a few realities which, because of their established existence, will come out the same way even in a different time and place. Diver's journeys to the past seem pathological because he makes them not so much to discover what went wrong or to finish unfinished situations as to savor the original idealist mistake. Because of perceptual and psychological mechanisms, he comes tragically close to these souls "sunk into eternal darkness" (197), close not just in sympathy but in essence.

The clearest illustration of this identification and the block it puts between Diver and professional help for his patients comes in his relationship with the American painter, transformed physically as well as psychically into "a living, agonizing sore," but a woman who "was coherent, even brilliant, within the limits of her special hallucinations" (199). To her terrible questions Diver responds with lies. Not only does he give her false hope, but, worse, he implies there is a cosmic justice which measures out pain according to an individual's actions. " 'Haven't you committed your share of petty sins and mistakes?" (200). Her breakdown remains obscure, but it connects to her attempt to challenge the male world, partly through her determination to paint. This episode, perhaps more than any other in *Tender Is the Night*, Fitzgerald distilled from his own life, directly from Zelda's suffering, which, circumstantially, flowed out of her obsessive and untimely dedication to ballet, and which came to distorted expression in her paintings:

> Your mother's utterly endless mulling and brooding over insolubles paved the way to her ruin. She had no education—not from lack of opportunity because she could have learned with

me—but from some inner stubbornness. She was a great original in her way, with perhaps a more intense flame at its highest than I ever had, but she tried and is still trying to solve all ethical and moral problems on her own, without benefit of the thousands dead.[5]

Her letters are tragically brilliant on all matters except those of central importance. How strange to have failed as a social creature—even criminals do not fail that way—they are the law's "Loyal Opposition," so to speak. But the insane are always mere guests on earth, eternal strangers carrying around broken decalogues that they cannot read.[6]

Zelda too "challenged men to battle" and tried to realize individuality through creative passion in art. But she could not reconcile the establishment of herself as a separate personality with the "thousands dead," or with history. She could not accept the necessary relationship between intelligence and creative purpose. She had to be *different,* but she did not see that separateness and uniqueness depend as much on *analogy* with other times and other persons as they do upon *contrast.*

But Diver's failure to answer honestly the anonymous woman's questions about reality, consciousness, and purpose again seems reflexive. He tells her that doubts and explorations could have led her not deeper into the country of life but only toward "a greater sickness." In addition, he invokes a regimen: " 'It's only by meeting the problems of every day, no matter how boring and trifling they seem, that you can make things drop into place again' " (210). Small order will bring cosmic order, small certainties larger ones. Diver is conscious of "lying" to her, conscious that the riddle of personality presents itself in all experience, and conscious that there is a relationship between perception and understanding, and one's actions. Indeed, the regimen he proposes has been his own during the enterprise of

[5] Andrew Turnbull, ed., *The Letters of F. Scott Fitzgerald* (New York: Charles Scribner's Sons, 1963), p. 78.
[6] *Ibid.,* p. 100.

the clinic. But beneath his formalized "round," few "things have dropped back into place again"—perhaps because, with Diver as with his patient, *the basic things never were in place.* In Diver's underground regions too " 'there's only confusion and chaos' " (201).

As Diver formulates the roots of the woman's predicament, one sees the source of his own difficulty: "The frontiers that artists must explore were not for her, ever. She was fine-spun, inbred—eventually she might find rest in some quiet mysticism. Exploration was for those with a measure of peasant blood, those with big thighs and thick ankles who could take punishment as they took bread and salt, on every inch of flesh and spirit" (201). Neither does Diver possess that outer and inner robustness he feels essential for explorations of the "frontiers of consciousness" (201). For that psychic and aesthetic dialectic which Keats called negative capability requires not merely a resilient double perception but faculties of mind and heart: it perhaps requires that creation be inseparable from an absolute commitment to survival. But with Diver, as with this ravaged artist, creation has become fatally mixed up with a still deeper need to be accepted, to be loved. "I am not loved; therefore I am not" is the condition perceived; "if I create, then I shall be admired" is the psychological formula for these fragile selves. Missing is that immediate and unquestioning contact with reality urged by a "measure of peasant blood." In its place is sheerly nervous energy spun out by the web of one's own tortured self. The afflicted woman now finds in herself no images fit for paint, but "only remote abstractions":

> As he arose the tears fled lava-like into her bandages.
> "That is for something," she whispered. "Something must come out of it."
> He stooped and kissed her forehead.
> "We must all try to be good," he said (201).

In place of the missing fragment, Diver doles out a moral imperative as vague and mysterious as her very illness. Finally, the scientist has become moralist, the psychiatrist minister, Dick Diver his father's moral self. For, as much as any patient, Diver has failed actively to discover himself—his nature, his past, and the relation of these things to his immediate context.

Like most events in *Escape*, Nicole's murderous relapse is less important for its own sake than for its perceptual vision. Moreover, the relationship between her hallucinations of Dick's infidelity and the facts is not simple and clear. Although Diver's statements (" 'This letter is deranged. . . . I had no relations of any kind with that girl. I didn't even like her' " [203]) are true, Nicole's suspicious impressions do penetrate below the level of fact to Dick's heart. Here, there is no such thing as objective reality; that is, one cannot reach or catalogue realities of consciousness (or, therefore, those external acts which follow) through logical, rational modes. Every personality, having its own subsets of desire, will necessarily create its own logic. Dick's growing coldness toward Nicole, for example, shows up best in the forms through which he chooses to relate to her. Scientific rationality substitutes for spontaneous affection and spontaneous resistance. The reverse also happens. When he should be a psychiatrist, he tends to act instead like the forgiving, loving husband. Roles, therefore, first invert and then become the reality they have displaced.

Certainly, guilt erodes Diver's detachment from Nicole's schizophrenia. Because of incomplete self-realization, he cannot distinguish between what he is and how he appears to Nicole: " 'It's always a delusion when I see what you don't want me to see.' He had a sense of guilt, as in one of those nightmares where we are accused of a crime which we recognize as something undeniably experienced, but which upon waking we realize we have not committed. *His eyes wavered from hers*" (206, my italics). I wake, therefore I am. Sleep and nightmares: desires and realities buried yet "unforgotten, unshriven, unexpurgated." Waking and thinking: the will's capacity to limit reality to immediate objects and time to one's present. Psychologically,

Diver's guilt is justified, particularly since his desires for women other than Nicole have not been acted out, but have been bottled up in his mind or, when begun to be acted out, as with Rosemary, curtailed by murder. So his unfaithfulness to Nicole would perpetuate guilt exactly because there is nothing tangible and fulfilled to regret. The denial of responsibility leads to the creation of guilt. Thus, when he feels Nicole as the "drought in the marrow of his bones," and when he can "not watch her disintegrations without participating in them," he is identifying with an object of his own horror in a particularly terrible way. When Nicole is seized with a spasm of madness, Diver experiences additional guilt because she, and not he, is suffering. He sees acted out in Nicole's divided self a process operative in the curtained recesses of himself. Eyes seeing in and out from shifting angles. And eyes giving external shapes and colors to demons and horrors escaped from within: "It was necessary to treat her with active and affirmative insistence, keeping the road to reality always open, making the road to escape harder going" (208). As the title, *Escape*, indicates, this is the dynamic according to which we judge Dick Diver, especially on his trip away from Nicole, away from the clinic, away, really, from his role of the last ten years. Is his "road to reality" a series of points joined only by sequence? Is his world flat, or are there destinations and changes of perspective and experience along its terrain?

3

Even to Dick's conscious self, this journey is an investigation of being; necessarily, he has "come away for his soul's sake" (218). But on that journey what does the soul take for focus and for direction? With an internalization of that love-work polarity which has split husband from psychiatrist, Fitzgerald shows the schism between two regions of Diver's mind: one "made up of the tawdry souvenirs of boyhood," the other detached and dry enough "to keep alive the low painful fire of intelligence" (212). Having escaped from Zurich, Diver's desires are diluted to fantasy dislocated from any real person in the past or present.

> Wolf-like under his sheep's clothing of long-staple Australian wool, he considered the world of pleasure—the incorruptible Mediterranean with sweet old dirt caked in the olive trees, the peasant girl near Savona with a face as green and rose as the color of an illuminated missal. He would take her in his hands and snatch her across the border . . .
>
> . . . but there he deserted her—he must press on toward the Isles of Greece, the cloudy waters of unfamiliar ports, the lost girl on shore, the moon of popular songs (211–12).

Even to himself, Diver's images drive out the possibilities of action. This is not even "love them and leave them," for there has been no loving. His sexuality has been released in a stream of prurient images revealing frightening changes in the dynamic of desire and its articulation. First, Diver had focused upon Rosemary, girl seeming to fulfill a prior image, but nevertheless touchable girl. Next appeared the unnamed girl at Gstaad whom he desired and rejected, this process going on mentally from a distance, but with real girl at least as reference point. Now there is no real girl; only his image of "the peasant girl near Savona," who possibly corresponds to a memory. Finally, his focus blurs into "the lost girl on shore." Girl, then, has been abstracted until she is almost a name held ready to ease Diver's feebler and feebler desire for contact with a woman. With Diver the male in such shape, how can the "low painful fire of intelligence" help the man? How can it do any more than make him aware, consciously, of the gulf between thought and action, desire and fulfillment? "Round, round, and round. Around forever." Not ratiocination but will is the faculty essential to any creative reversal of self-direction for Diver.

Likewise, where history is concerned, Diver seems increasingly a mere spectator. Having heard of Abe North's squalid death, he awakens in Munich to lines of German veterans paying tribute to their dead: "It was a long column of men in uniform, wearing the familiar helmet of 1914, thick men in frock coats and silk hats; burghers, aristocrats, plain men. It was a society of veterans going to lay wreaths on the tombs of the dead. The column marched slowly with a sort of swagger for a lost magnificence, a past effort, a forgotten sorrow. The faces were only formally sad, but Dick's lungs burst for a moment with regret for Abe's death, and his own youth of ten years ago" (217). Casualties will breed casualties, disaster total disaster, for swagger will evolve to goose step. As yet, though, all is unchanged. These surviving Germans whose efforts were simultaneously humiliated and vindicated at Versailles try to turn present into past through the twin bonds of brotherhood and nationhood. Diver, on the other hand, is an individual psychic casualty. Having had no direct connection with whatever "lost magnificence" there was to World War I, his personality disintegrates outside those public events and historical tragedies which link these former soldiers to a reality and history larger than themselves. Diver, however, has nothing but his own misunderstood experience as context for the casualty of Abe's death and his own abstraction from history. Without any clear, continuous relation to his own history, Diver mistakenly envies the bond among these Germans. At any rate, he has no context but unconnected memories—he must move on.

At Innsbruck, next stop on Diver's imperial road to Rome, the setting is monastic. Surrounded by relics, not the least of which is Abe North and his forgotten music, Diver must take self-inventory. For he has been changed from a creative clinical and theoretical psychiatrist to operator and stand-in owner of a clinic from which he has had to flee. The other falling off— spurred on by his blunted purpose—involves his willingness to allow money to define identity. But the utter paralysis flows less from the dilemma, from the flaws and failures in themselves, than from Diver's response to his situation: " 'I've wasted nine years teaching the rich the ABC's of human decency, but

I'm not done. I've got too many unplayed trumps in my hand' "
(219). If Diver were weaning the rich away from a singular
cultural neurosis, one might grant him his claims about the
civilizing process. For in such a case the problem itself would
inspire and sustain a certain energy and commitment, and the
outcome would be consistent with psychiatry as a humanizing
vocation. Beyond these things, one gasps at Diver's self-delu-
sions. Which "human" decencies? How can a man's soul and
integrity progressively be sucked out of him by the very personalities he leads to sensibility and humanity? Certainly, there is
a terrific hubris here. Diverted from his ambitions in psychiatry,
diverted to adolescent fantasies, Diver now perversely revels
in the treadmill dance of the past nine years. Aware that his
own promising explorations into "the frontiers of consciousness"
have ceased, he persuades himself that his life and vocation
have shaped some active social purpose beyond that of preserving, in part, his wife's sanity.

But upon the next human contact, the next opportunity to
act out his obsessive desires, Diver's bravado dissolves into the
same paralysis. Noticing an attractive woman, solitary like himself, Diver cannot make advances or even talk to her. In fact,
the ease of the situation, the woman's tacit approval, "kept
worrying him." What is it, after all, but a mask, of which she
approves? "Why," he moralizes (and rationalizes), "when I
could have had a good share of the pretty women of my time
for the asking, why start that now? With a wraith, with a fragment of my desire? Why?" (220, my italics). The asking process, the male demand, is, of course, what he has never faced.
Even woman as daughter—Nicole and Rosemary—has had to
seek him and to *ask* him. Now, uncharacteristically, Diver answers his evasive rhetorical queries. His statement-metaphor:
"the old asceticism, the *actual* unfamiliarity triumphed" (220,
my italics). Yet, as Dick once wondered of Franz, we must wonder of him: what end does this asceticism advance—other than
repression and self-loathing? Somehow it seems to urge disci-

pline and form (read as abstinence) for their own sakes in the false conviction that what Dick Diver needs is, simply, to work. He, in this justification, allows himself to slide away from realities of body and consciousness, just as in his counsel he had euphemized the scabbed woman's honest questions about her reality.

Voluntarily, Diver makes no attempt to confront critically, and therefore perhaps therapeutically, his own past, but his father's abrupt death interrupts his preoccupation with loneliness and opens up that past to whose authority and values he has been so loyal. Like Nick Carraway, Diver views social qualities as moral values. Genteel form, after all, can be almost as effective a way of prospering as the wholesale hardware business. In fact, Diver's recollection of his father's "good heart" is followed by the clergyman's own moral of the accommodation to power. " 'After that,' " he says of his deference to a hostess, " 'I made many friends in that town' " (221). Diver still cannot separate love for his father from allegiance to the maxim that "nothing could be superior to 'good instincts,' honor, courtesy, and courage" (221); nor does he distinguish these qualities from the different demands of his own experience and historical context. Indeed, he calls to mind Oswald Spengler's analysis of the absolute mode governing Western thought:

> It is *this* that is lacking to the Western thinker, the very thinker in whom we might have expected to find it—insight into the *historically relative* character of his data, which are expressions of *one specific existence and one only*; knowledge of the necessary limits of their validity; the conviction that his "unshakable" truths and "eternal" views are simply true for him and eternal for his world view; the duty of looking beyond them to what the men of the other Cultures have with equal certainty evolved out of themselves.[7]

[7] Oswald Spengler, *The Decline of the West*, vol. I, trans. Charles Francis Atkinson (New York: Alfred A. Knopf, 1926–28), p. 17.

Spengler's accusation is particularly telling if we apply his relative method to different traditions within Diver's Western culture.

Relative perspective has become the crucial aesthetic issue here because of attempts (Richard Lehan presents the fullest case) to identify Fitzgerald with Diver, not simply through particulars of biography, but in essential vision. It is true that in a recollection of his father Fitzgerald confessed that "always deep in my subconscious I have referred judgments back to him, what he would have thought or done." [8] But this is not to say he had no critical perspective on his emotional dependence or upon that experienced by the characters in his novels. At any rate, he verifies this process when he remarks in a letter written to his cousin Ceci a month or two after his father's death: "Sometimes I think of Father, but only sentimentally." [9] When judgment would be harsh on parents, sentiment, even sentimentality, has a place, but Fitzgerald's two responses and their closeness in time suggest that through negative capability the novelist and the man in him could render and at the same time stay detached from an uncritical response to a highly charged emotional experience.

In 1940 with the world falling down around him, Fitzgerald again reflected upon his father and his family, upon that ancestral generation, in a way that suggests the double perspective operating in relation to character Dick Diver in 1933–34:

> With Father, Uncle John and Aunt Elise a generation goes. I wonder how deep the Civil War was in them—that odd childhood on the border between the states with Grandmother and old Mrs. Scott and the shadow of Mrs. Suratt. What a sense of honor and duty—almost eighteenth century rather than Victoria. How lost they seemed in the changing world—my father

[8] F. Scott Fitzgerald, "The Death of My Father," *The Apprentice Fiction of F. Scott Fitzgerald, 1909–1917*, ed. John Kuehl (New Brunswick: Rutgers University Press, 1965), p. 67.

[9] Turnbull, ed., *Letters of F. Scott Fitzgerald*, p. 410.

and Aunt Elise struggling to keep their children in the *haute bourgeoisie* when their like were sinking into obscure farm life or being lost in the dark boarding houses in Georgetown.[10]

Awe there certainly is of another time's "sense of honor and duty," but keeping pace is an intelligence which knows that, like the twentieth-century American system supporting Nicole Warren, this *haute bourgeoisie* society contained within itself its own doom. Moreover, in this morally and politically self-destroying Gilded Age culture, "honor and duty" became qualities finally as rote and abstract as the lace curtains of those immigrant Irish who seemed to raise themselves to genteel status. They became qualities bound up with a myth about personality and society, a myth which historical process has shown to have served white supremacy, class exploitation, and culture for the privileged. So it is that Dick Diver has a fatal attraction to the aristocracy his father failed to reach, and so did his delusion hallucinate the merger of Warren money and Diver sensibility. But Scott Fitzgerald, writing in penury at decrepit Ellerslie, understood this; Fitzgerald sends Diver back to Buffalo not, as Lehan says, "in search of the father," but as an exile without home or connection anywhere.[11] Or, since these purposes are not incompatible, surely Fitzgerald himself knew the lost father was not to be found—not in any case as a source of nourishment.

For all his identification with his dead father, Diver's true return to his own and a deeper ancestral past occurs only in the interior of America. His relation to place typifies Fitzgerald's vision of how Americans do deal with their past and with the issue of continuity. In New York harbor, the approach to America, Diver senses the homeland, but the city itself appears only as a "magnificent facade," with the implication, like Carraway's in *Gatsby*, that America herself lies "somewhere back in

[10] *Ibid.*, pp. 419–20.
[11] Richard Lehan, *F. Scott Fitzgerald and the Craft of Fiction* (Carbondale: Southern Illinois University Press, 1967), p. 177.

vast obscurity beyond the city where the dark fields of the republic rolled on under the night" (137). Here, as with Carraway, the death of a man rouses Diver to explore his connections to America, as that continent sought out by a race of men determined to re-create themselves through a new society. Deliberately, Fitzgerald keeps Diver out of touch with the continent and its accompanying history as he stops in Buffalo— a commercial, pioneering town, a middle-western town—for his father's body. Diver soars with a "spirit of place," a connection with authority and continuity, only when he journeys backward in time and space to those dead generations who had settled Virginia over three hundred years ago: "Only as the local train shambled into the low-forested clayland of Westmoreland County did he feel once more identified with his surroundings; at the station he saw a star he knew, and a cold moon bright over Chesapeake Bay; he heard the rasping wheels of buckboards turning, the lovely fatuous voices, the sound of sluggish primeval rivers flowing softly under soft Indian names" (222). Here are connections between imagination and reality unspecified in *The Great Gatsby's* vision of primal America. As history recedes, we arrive at an interval when the continent seemed briefly to hold together white settlers and Indians. For once, Diver does not merely see; he hears, and is alive to whatever life and sensations linger upon this land. Robert McAlmon's paraphrase of the *Contact* "Manifesto" of 1920 may suggest, as an American version of Lawrence's "spirit of place," the kind of national identity which Fitzgerald, no longer an exile, was trying to evoke. American prose, McAlmon thought, should both render and create "the essential contact between words and the locality that breeds them, in this case America." [12]

Having buried his displaced father, Dick Diver takes imaginative note of the continuity between settlers and the land in early colonial days: "Dick had no more ties here and did not believe

[12] Robert E. Knoll, ed., *Robert McAlmon and the Lost Generation* (Lincoln: University of Nebraska Press, 1962), p. 134.

he would come back. He knelt on the hard soil. These dead, he knew them all, their weather-beaten faces with blue flashing eyes, the spare violent bodies, the souls made of new earth in the forest-heavy darkness of the seventeenth century. 'Good-bye, my father—good-bye, all my fathers' " (222). No transient Dutch sailors were these men. Nor does Dick Diver allude to an instant real and verified but then delusionally repeated forever within men, to that archetypal "transitory enchanted moment," historical to begin with and then falsely eternalized in myth. No, Diver and Fitzgerald refer to an early society of those who settled in America and committed themselves to build "a living homeland," to obey in relation to this continent "some deep, inward voice of religious belief," as D. H. Lawrence articulated the choices in "The Spirit of Place." "Men," Lawrence continued, "are free when they belong to a living, organic, *believing* community, active in fulfilling some unfulfilled, perhaps unrealized purpose. Not when they are escaping to some wild west." [13] What compels one to these men, individually, is their physical vitality, their ability to "take punishment as they took bread and salt, on every inch of flesh and spirit" (201). One responds also to the rare presence in them of the tie that binds one generation to another. Of these early Americans one cannot say, as de Tocqueville did of American men in the nineteenth century, that "every man there readily loses all trace of the ideas of his forefathers or takes no care about them." [14]

The imperative, generally in America, as it is for Dick Diver, is a living relationship between past and present, between continuity and consciousness. In his study, "Oedipus and the Serpent," Wolfgang Lederer has written of the dynamic opposition essential to the transition from boy to man. During a son's

---

[13] D. H. Lawrence, *Studies in Classic American Literature* (New York: Viking Press, 1964), p. 6.

[14] Alexis de Tocqueville, *Democracy in America*, vol. 2 (New York: Alfred A. Knopf, 1945), p. 4.

struggle to identity, Lederer contends, his "negative feelings create the new order; the positive feelings assure a measure of continuity." [15] Again, in America's context, de Tocqueville's observations record the historical opposite of Lederer's polarity:

> It would be an error to suppose that this [manhood] is preceded by a domestic struggle in which the son has obtained by a sort of moral violence the liberty that his father has refused him. . . . The father foresees the limits of his authority long beforehand, and when the time arrives, *he surrenders it without a struggle*; the son looks forward to the exact period at which he will be *his own master*, and he enters upon his freedom with precipitation and *without effort*, as a possession which is his own and which no one seeks to wrest from him.[16]

Can a boy's manhood be served up to him in such gratuitous fashion? How shall such sons shape themselves? From what roots will they toughen and grow? "Under Ben Bulben," Yeats's epitaph for self, race, and culture, asserts a necessary relationship between struggle, upheaval, and the action of maturity:

> Even the wisest man grows tense
> With *some sort* of violence
> Before he can accomplish fate,
> Know his work or choose his mate.[17]

Is it any wonder that when weak or absent American fathers cheated their sons of the Oedipal battle, those sons—their energies displaced from men and women to an expansionist impulse often aggressive toward the land—wandered into an abstract future? Denied the battle of the generations whose changing poles of authority are vital to the motion of history, such sons considered all time blank because, for them, the past

[15] Wolfgang Lederer, "Oedipus and the Serpent," *Psychoanalytic Review*, vol. 51, no. 4 (Winter, 1964–65), p. 57.

[16] de Tocqueville, *Democracy in America*, pp, 203–4. My italics.

[17] W. B. Yeats, "Under Ben Bulben," *The Collected Poems of W. B. Yeats* (New York: Macmillan, 1956), p. 342. My italics.

had been without continuity. In "The Death of My Father,"
Fitzgerald, with a son's sympathy and an adult's intelligence,
defined his own father's predicament in similar terms: "I did
not understand at all why men that I knew were vulgar and not
gentlemen made him stand up or give the better chair on the
verandah. But I know now. There was a new young peasant
stock coming up every ten years & he was of the generation of
the colonies and the revolution." [18] Dick Diver too—with him
Fitzgerald's detachment is clearer—suffers from a father who
set in motion for his son not an identity flowing from the ten-
sions between new strength and continuities, but one fitted
together from manners and appearances: how things looked.
Only in fantasy can Diver's journey take him back to "the generation of the colonies and the revolution," or back beyond that
to ancestors with "souls made of new earth in the forest-heavy
darkness of the seventeenth century."

Fitzgerald imagines too a process of creation between Diver's
ancestors and the land they inhabit. When he speaks of their
evolving souls, he alludes to a new *Genesis* in a definite, never
to be repeated, historical time and place. These men were
formed by a union between the "new earth" of America, this
continent's unknown, its "forest-heavy darkness," and the intellectual and theological bonds of Calvinism which were loosening
the ties to old authorities, old potencies of kingship and fatherhood. But the allusion to this early Virginia colony does not
evoke what Lawrence called an unfree "breaking away from all
dominion." [19] Here, unlike the *Genesis* myth, these men come
alive from the very authority of the earth itself. Unemphasized
is any God-like creator. No, something in the spirit of the land
and in the historical moment organically sprang these men to
new life and consciousness. And that new life did not cease with
the seventeenth century. For it was Westmoreland County
which, whatever the deficiences of the American Revolution,

18 Kuehl, ed., *The Apprentice Fiction of F. Scott Fitzgerald*, p. 68.
19 Lawrence, *Studies in Classic American Literature*, p. 7.

did produce men like George Washington who energized a people to its independent and experimental destiny as a free nation.

Dick Diver's benediction as he leaves for good ("Good-bye, my father—good-bye, all my fathers") raises the vital question about America, the discontinuity of its generations, and finally, about American history. How, in individuals and society, was the cleavage rent between those first fathers and the last? The Laurentian vision has its truth. Contact between men, between men and women, between man and nature has become less immediate and more and more mechanical and abstract, more and more dependent upon euphemism and vicarious experience. Thus Diver's father, himself one of the uprooted, a Southerner come north after the Civil War, substituted a corrupt and illusory code—legend—for active grappling with an unknown place and a difficult, transitional period—history. Instead, perhaps like Dan Cody in *Gatsby*, he handed Northerners with drab lives and halfway guilty consciences a Southern, chivalric reading of American history which prevented them and him from facing both their own passivity and that violence and chaos concealed beneath their ideals of historical action. Such euphemism not only distorts the truth; it also prevents one and one's descendants from having to deal with the facts as they present themselves in the truth that is denied.

4

Diver departs from Virginia and from America, but, fatherless, where will he go? From what authority, what vision, will he live and act? Having overleapt a failed father to self-reliant ancestral fathers, will he be able to transfer their ancient virility to himself in the twentieth century? His reaffirmed exile suggests not. For he must leave this place—only in racial memory are its roots his—and continue his journey into a more individual, psychic past. Once in Rome, destination of the old imperial road, Diver manipulates things so that he meets, cir-cumstantially, "the person he had come to see, the person for whom he had made the Mediterranean crossing" (224). Upon seeing Rosemary, Diver's conscious and unconscious selves come together, perhaps for the first time in the novel. She, whom he has desired and denied, then resought in anonymous images, he acknowledges through actual contact. True to his break with all contexts—those of his two pasts in America and that of Warren-bought, aristocratic exile—he wishes none for Rosemary. Even more radically than with Nicole ten years be-fore, "he wanted to hold her eloquent giving of herself in its precious shell, till he enclosed it, till it no longer existed out-side him" (225). Lacking an integrated self of his own and fearful that the pieces will be scattered Osiris fashion, Diver must incorporate and therefore deny individuation to the wom-an he possesses sexually. Mythically, he carries the Adam and Eve archetype to its extreme. Eve, who has been made flesh from the word of the dreaming Adam, now must return to his personality because he can no longer survive without the miss-ing rib.

At the same time Diver knows that Rosemary has become a person in her own right; he knows too that the four years since 1925 have shifted the leverage in the father-daughter paradigm to Rosemary. As they explore each other sexually, it is now Rosemary who defines the action: " 'No, not now— these things are rhythmic' " (228), defines it when she is not answering phone calls to do with her career and with other lovers. For the demands Diver makes upon her reinforce for Rosemary the ideal mode through which she had been per-ceiving him. "She did not want him to be like other men, yet here were the same exigent demands, as if he wanted to take some of herself away, carry it off in his pocket" (229). Until the father-daughter framework is re-established, she does not make either a physical or a psychological surrender.

Finally the drama of their affair drowns out their passion just as in Rosemary's current movie, *The Grandeur That Was Rome*, the set of the forum is "larger than the forum itself" (230). Rosemary seems far more concerned with her sex appeal on film than in her personal life. Generally, neither personality nor history has any validity or integrity in its own right; rather, each is the property of the movie industry, an industry obedient to and increasingly responsible for mass taste and vision. The particular actors in Rosemary's company may well be "people of bravery and industry" (231)—as young Dick Diver was a dedicated psychiatrist—but these gifts are viciously degraded by the film industry which flourishes by pandering to a nation's self-justifying notions of greatness. For the democratic illusion insists that all Americans are implicated in greatness, whether or not this greatness is desirable, moral, or even real. As director, Monroe Stahr explains to the English novelist Boxley in *The Last Tycoon*, Hollywood's democratic " 'condition is that we have to take people's favorite folklore and dress it up and give it back to them' " (105).

Meanwhile, Rome, its historical vibrations everywhere, provides a background to the clash of values going on within Dick Diver. Before the seduction is accomplished, he and Rosemary dine "in a high-terraced villa overlooking the ruined forum of an undetermined period of the decadence" (231). In this ruined space, time blurs; moral and civilized values dissolve once republic is perverted to empire. " 'Do you know what these old Roman families are?' " Diver later asks the complacent Collis Clay. " 'They're bandits, they're the ones who got possession of the temples and palaces after Rome went to pieces and preyed on the people' " (239). Such bluntness and clarity on Rome's decadence and its spoils system makes one wonder why Diver has not an equally well-developed perception of the changes wrought in America during its transition from republic to empire. At any rate the values whose presence in Rome Diver attacks—arrogance, self-gratification, prurience—are qualities which with Rosemary and during his stay here he cannot resist.

Rosemary's sexual history, in as many particulars as possible, fascinates him more than the girl herself. It's as if, fearful of genuine love and contact, Dick must belittle even the little emotion and passion between them. For he is able to separate himself from Rosemary only after hearing from her own lips of her seduction by other men. Indeed a "spoiled priest," Dick wants only to hear tales of sin; his powers of compassion have long fled him. Fittingly, Rosemary's continued contact with the young Italian Nicotera provokes Dick—"Because youth called to youth"—to jealousy and racial insults. At the crisis point Diver returns to his old psychological paternal ownership of Rosemary. His hold on her is not that of a lover so much as it is that of the father whose feelings, because of happy childhood memories, she cannot bear to hurt. What Diver requires is her total submergence to his identity, but the identity she had adored was the composite mask of his father's genteel, chivalric "good instincts," not the jealous, paranoid, self-doubting man who stands before her in Rome. In short, even if Diver could reject the paternal values, he has no other attractive instincts with which to replace the old.

Unhappy, divided between old loyalties and the course of her career and her life, Rosemary, like the anonymous, mad painter, asks Dick to bring to consciousness their condition and life's condition.

> "Oh, such a shame, such a shame. Oh, such a shame. What's it all about anyhow?"
> "I've wondered for a long time."
> "But why bring it to me?"
> "I guess I'm the Black Death," he said slowly. "I don't seem to bring people happiness anymore" (237).

First psychiatrist and now man have abdicated the responsibility of articulate consciousness. The "it," insoluble reality, is brought to Rosemary by Dick, not as a necessary element in life, but as the plague, as death. The doctor who should heal sick souls, the man who has given back to others "their best selves"—now this personality has become himself a fatal and contagious disease.

Diver's metaphor of the Black Death becomes immediately operative in his experience, as a self-fulfilling prophecy which corrodes further his own decaying self. The contagious touch turns inward. Rejecting with deception Rosemary's invitation for a last night together, Diver's energy turns aggressive and truculent toward Italians, toward Collis Clay, but above all toward himself. Once more he hunts for "that special girl" among nightclub strangers. This last search is particularly damning, for he has just refused contingent sexuality, apparently because it did involve a woman also a person in her own right, and because it brought to the surface the guilt he seems to transfer from his dream image to the real woman when encountered in the flesh. The strange girl his unsuppressible desires now fix on is "a young English girl, with blonde hair and a healthy, pretty English face," but, most of all, given his neurosis, a girl who "smiled at him again with an invitation he understood, that denied the flesh even in the act of tendering it" (240). Even when present in the flesh, word remains word for Diver.

As if the fumes from his "black heart" were not stifling enough, Diver goes outside where "a marshy vapor from the Campagna, a sweat of exhausted cultures tainted the air" (242). In a fight with some taxi drivers, Diver's manhood, long in bondage to "exhausted" values, surfaces in open rebellion. But as a man of violence, Diver fails as thoroughly as he has in his other guises—psychiatrist, husband, paramour—and for some of the same perceptual reasons. Pathetically, he invokes a tradition that totally ignores the particular present context: "The passionate impatience of the week leaped up in Dick and clothed itself like a flash in violence, the honorable, the traditional resource of his land; he stepped forward and clapped the man's face" (243). Neither about himself nor about America does he perceive the relationship between repression and aggression, and violence. In fact, that American past of men facing each other in fair, formalized violence is more imagined than real. The ambush is a more American form than the duel. But in any case, this ritual gesture, this duel form will not suffice. Diver is in a street fight; he is not back on the Mason-Dixon line defending Southern culture or white virginity. One might say too that, in terms of his lineage, Diver now is called to reckoning for the American transformation of lies to illusions. His own naive understanding of the nature of violence follows, in part, from the glorification of ancestral violence—Mad Anthony Wayne— into heroic formulae like "the honorable, the traditional resource of his land." Diver, deferred—that very word suggests temporary escape—from active service in World War I, did not learn the lesson written in the blood and bones of the physical casualties of the war and recorded by Ernest Hemingway in *A Farewell to Arms:* "There were many words that you could not stand to hear and finally only the names of places had dignity. Certain numbers were the same way and certain dates and these with the names of places were all you could say and then have them mean anything. Abstract words such as glory, honor, courage, or hallow were obscene beside the concrete names of villages, the numbers of roads, the names of rivers, the numbers of regiments and the dates." [20]

The Italian soul will have its "glory, honor, and courage"; Mussolini's boys will see to it, but with clubs and fists and boots instead of with words. World War I had been the end of words for despised peoples and nations. Diver's fantasies have buckled against concrete violence; out of this he loses consciousness and regains it helpless enough to do what is a greater humiliation: beseech Baby Warren for help.

Jeered and hissed by loiterers who mistake him for the rapist-murderer of a five-year-old child, Diver perversely, but in a sense truly, assumes the weight of the crime. " 'I want to make a

[20] Ernest Hemingway, *A Farewell to Arms* (New York: Charles Scribner's Sons, 1929), p. 185.

speech,' Dick cried. 'I want to explain to these people how I raped a five-year-old girl. Maybe I did'" (253). Guilt is universal; we are all guilty, even if we do not know of what crime, but in a specific way this real child, raped and slain, externalizes the incest horror which presumably haunts Dick Diver. During this interval he had seduced Rosemary, who seemed to him the actualization of his dream image, taken her and seen himself as the Black Death, as a lover who communicated a psychological plague, if no other. Now we have Diver wanting to confess to a grotesque, fully horrible act of violation. Thus, if there has come into being a "new self," it seems to delight in things criminal. On the other hand, the apparent absurdity of Diver's confession serves to conceal the guilt he feels and the dissociation that now exists between him and an old order at last exposed as sick unto death, as a cultural Black Death.

This "escape" process has severed Diver from any self-realization which would allow him to act upon other personalities and upon the world. He has no more center. Psychologically, Baby Warren is correct when she decides that "whatever Dick's previous record was, they [the power in the world of *Tender Is the Night* is indeed held by the theys, anonymous, impersonal, and impervious] now possessed a moral superiority over him for as long as he proved of any use" (253). Like Carraway, Diver's morality has consisted more of socially serving manners than of commitment to honesty, integrity, and self-respect as self-inclusive values for human personality. On this level of manners —how personalities and relationships seem, rather than what they are—he has been caught violating his own code. According to his own rules as well as those of the system he serves, Diver is used up and, therefore, expendable. In 1929, his value as a "capital investment" has crashed precipitously below the margin required for the Warren fortune to sustain him.

eight

The Way Home: "But here there is no light"

1

"Of all natural forces," Scott Fitzgerald wrote in *The Crack-Up*, "vitality is the incommunicable one," and, he might have added, the quality most essential to survival and to power over history.[1] To explain the transfer of dominion from Dick Diver to Tommy Barban at the end of *Tender Is the Night*, one is tempted to propose a male version of Henry Adams's notion of the evolution of historical energy from virgin to dynamo. As the idealist with his ideas, his moral instincts, and, finally, his reading of history as lost, romantic myth, Diver resembles the decaying virgin; whereas Barban, his driving, kinetic energy and magnetism put behind edifice and stratagem, behind the material structures which concretize a culture, often seems more like impersonal dynamo than flesh-and-blood man. Diver's failure, and the failure of the idealist generally, is a failure of tough and sensuous energy, just as Barban's failure, and the failure of plundering, animal-rational man, is the failure of sensibility and tenderness.

The old order that passes away at the end of *Tender Is the Night* is not any order of aristocracy, not the leisure class or its supporting system. What disappears from the stage of history

---

[1] F. Scott Fitzgerald, *The Crack-Up*, ed. Edmund Wilson (New York: New Directions, 1945), p. 74.

and culture are Dick Diver and the social and psychological sub-limations for which he stands. His illusory and historically vicious " 'good instincts'—honor, courtesy, and courage" black out, as does the conviction that sensibility and aesthetic con-templation can create personalities greater than any sum of their parts. Or, as Fitzgerald himself later said of Diver's values and their mode, "he is after all a sort of superman, an approximation of the *hero* seen in overcivilized terms—taste is no substitute for vitality but in the book it has to do duty for it." [2]

Because *Tender Is the Night*'s great subject has been person-ality and the historical, psychological, and perceptual forces which shape it, form in *The Way Home* takes its cue from the changes in these relationships. Of Diver the individual, for ex-ample, it almost had to be aesthetically decided that "from now on he is mystery man, at least to Nicole with her guessing at the mystery." [3] As his values fade out of his world, Diver's reflective perspective ceases. Increasingly, "his own story" is "spinning out inside him"; no longer can he acknowledge, let alone provide, moral and social guidelines. Nicole, for her part, cannot afford many speculations about Dick's fate. Her leap to a new self requires fracture of her loyalty to both Dick's values and the mode of manners which had enforced them. For her metamor-phosis to have wholeness, complexity must be sacrificed. Reality cannot have layer after layer, substratum below stratum for its truth. As Diver dives into his sea chambers and Nicole emerges whole on the shore of the world, the facts become more and more expressive of personality. And I mean facts in the crudest, simplest form. Nicole's new self and her dynastic consolidation through marriage to Barban are reductive states. With power, money, and metallic sensibility for voice, she and he scorn all density, all complexity. And just as facts express Nicole's me-

[2] Andrew Turnbull, ed., *The Letters of F. Scott Fitzgerald* (New York: Charles Scribner's Sons, 1963), p. 567.
[3] Fitzgerald's sketch for *Tender Is the Night*, Appendix 3, Arthur Mizener, *The Far Side of Paradise* (Boston: Houghton Mifflin, 1965), p. 352.

chanical existence, the facts alone—events, objects, gestures—will have to stimulate us to judgments about the meaning of Diver's end.

At the end of *The Great Gatsby*, Fitzgerald used language to extend the American dream to Western history. The elements of narrowness and trivality in Gatsby's story and the novel's context made overstatement the vehicle for Carraway's universal vision. In *Tender Is the Night* the aesthetic situation is reversed. There, the promise of Diver had been so real, the historical-cultural background so complexly stated and restated, the waste so inevitable, the only way to rouse us further is to pretend that nothing has happened at all. The aesthetic dynamics of the "dying fall" involve, as Fitzgerald explained to Hemingway, "telling the reader in the last pages that, after all, this is just a casual event, and trying to let *him* come to bat for *me* rather than going out to shake his nerves, whoop him up, then leaving him rather in the condition of a frustrated woman in bed." [4] Climax, then, is a two-way street, a natural event that, with reader or with woman, cannot be imposed by will or by force. Understatement during the coda to *Tender Is the Night* should arouse us to protest. We should protest and resist, not so much Diver's fate, but the possibility that his destiny is our own—inevitably, repetitively.

Tragedy of a noncathartic variety—the cathartic vision seems to me an aesthetic way of upholding the established order, the existing cultural values, with *Oedipus Rex* the prototype—involves a peculiar form of horror. Its horror comes not from the facts of madness, annihilation, and chaos but more from the lack of any voice, any perspective that can arrange reality's fragments in some way, no matter how temporary. In Dick Diver dissolution is horrible because it results from the very context and consciousness now incapable of articulation. His values make him a casualty of chaos and bring to us a closed circle of perception. What difference does it make where he is, whom he is

4 Turnbull, ed., *Letters of F. Scott Fitzgerald*, p. 310.

with, or what he thinks and does? What difference does it make that he is no one? If Fitzgerald, by pretending none of these things makes any difference, stirs our discontent, then it will be our imperative to shape appropriate values into a humane society. For the one irreducible given of *Tender Is the Night* is that no individual can develop, creatively or otherwise, in isolation. The chickens of history will come home to roost; no human coop, whether in Europe, or Hollywood, or the Finger Lakes, is free from visitation.

2

In *The Way Home* Fitzgerald changes the dominant way of seeing from *Escape*'s mode of reflective complexity to one where externals undermine and devour the impressions arranged by consciousness over long intervals. Often the question is not so much what is true as whether truth, falsely arrived at, can have any integrity. Kathe and Franz Gregorovius, for example, argue mechanically about whether Diver's unhealed scars are the result of a debauch or shipboard boxing. This innocuous argument becomes perceptually sinister because of the relationship between fact and conclusion. If Kathe can persuade Franz that Dick has " 'been on a debauch,' " then Franz will leapfrog to the judgment that " 'Dick is no longer a serious man' " (258– 59). The fact that this conclusion does not follow from the mere fact of a debauch does not deter Franz from persuading himself that "he had *never* thought" "that Dick was a serious person" (259, my italics). Thus do facts long-denied become, when acknowledged, instruments of absolute reduction which in their own turn deny facts, the fluid, complex facts of experience held in common.

More and more, personality becomes unequal to unexpected pressures. In Lausanne, Diver finds his profession inadequate to the likes of Francisco, the young nobleman homosexual, and his personal resources inadequate to the extra tenderness Nicole requires after her father re-enters and departs from their path. Indeed, life generally has about it an accidental and random quality. This sense of life as unpredictable, since it follows Diver's previous capacity to direct out of the ruins of experience coherent dramas and shows, leads the Divers toward immobility. It's as if now they are at the drama rather than its shapers and participants. To each other they are fast becoming artifacts. "Someone had brought a phonograph into the bar and they sat listening to 'The Wedding of the Painted Doll' " (269). Together and singly, they begin to look to the world to decide their destiny. Nor is it entirely clear to which forces they yield up power over their lives.

At this imprecise point, Diver's meditation about the odd and different breeding grounds of charm carries him, imperceptibly, into *The Way Home*'s subject: the changes in personality structure emerging in the clash between consciousness and the twentieth century:

> Dick tried to dissect it into pieces small enough to store away, realizing that the totality of a life may be different in quality from its segments, and also that life during one's late thirties seemed capable of being observed only in segments. His love for Nicole and Rosemary, his friendship with Abe North, with Tommy Barban in the broken universe of the war's ending—in such contacts the personalities had seemed to press up so close to him that he became the personality itself; there seemed some necessity of taking all or nothing; it was as if for the remainder of his life he was condemned to carry with him the egos of certain people, early met and early loved, and to be only as complete as they were complete themselves (263).

> "You're not a romantic philosopher—you're a scientist. Memory, force, character—especially good sense. That's going to be your trouble—judgment about yourself" (5).

What Diver is talking about, and what the Rumanian intellectual had warned him about in 1916, is individuation. Neither as scientist nor as romantic philosopher can Dick Diver put all the pieces together again. Not only is personality composed of disjointed segments, but Diver, even though he is a scientist, can no longer conceive even of *observing* it in wholes. Like a romantic philosopher, he is willing to grant totality to a given life; but he regards his own life, fifteen years after his vision of complexity and wholeness, as somehow incompatible with any composite perception. Indeed, as he refers to "the broken universe of the war's ending," he includes all of his generation in his predicament. Personality structures seemingly integrated by experience, background, and vision flew apart in the war's explosion, and the fragments, assembled again from different directions, could not fit the niches of the old formations. As disintegrations of cultural and political forms increased—the former leaderless, the latter in search of *Duce* or *Führer*—historical chaos externalized the collapse, within individuals, of those psychological networks which, woven together, had formed whatever totalities make a being greater than the sum of its parts. But Diver calls into doubt the notion, central to integration, that the dynamic personality supersedes its segments. For him all that is graspable are separate segments of reality and of self.

What petrifies Diver's broken parts, however, is his inability to shed the egos of those close to him. Not only does he carry, inseparable from his own, "the egos of certain people, early met and early loved," but, in total dependence, he can then "be only as complete as they were complete themselves." In addition, we are talking about the chaos of contrary egos pulling centrifugally at Diver's weakening core. Ultimately, the flypaper will be captured by the flies. We must, to refer the matter to physics, contrast Diver's refractory relationship with others to Nicole's reflective (mirror-image) mode of being. For given intervals she will become one person or another, but no roots accompany these changes of self. Nicole reflects, mirrors other egos, then sheds them, as a tough and independent actress might her roles. Others are no weight, no resistant and clinging substance to Nicole as they are to Dick. Hers is both a pure and shallow contingency of personality. No doubt this is partly due to the solidity and permanence of her history, just as Dick's confusion about the relationship between himself and the qualities of others suggests the crippling partition in his own past between form and action. Diver cannot separate fact from idealized personal and historical memories; for him, personality knows the world through incorporation. Given his past, his mere ingestion of others is simultaneously an act of self-terror and of heroic confidence. History a vanishing memory, Diver is never sure that there is a world open to him, whereas Nicole, sure of her history, can fortify herself through the mirror of others because unconsciously she knows that the ongoing energy of her history will pulverize whatever memories linger of guilt and nonexistence.

Unsure of who and what he is, Dick Diver founds his identity upon others' admiration, an admiration caused and complicated by the fact that he, like Jay Gatsby, reflects back to the admirers the same selves they wish to believe in—their best selves. But what does the loved one do with such admiration? There seems little power within him to break down and absorb in different form the egos of those "early met and early loved." Having no living roots, he must rely on others' substance to form his ideals of self. Having long ago chosen heroic uniqueness over historical individuation, Diver must seduce others into admiration, for he needs the totalities of other selves to enlarge his own epic dimensions. And the most horrifying and crippling characteristic is the "necessity of taking all or nothing," which I would connect to Diver's psychological and historical idealism. After all, the creator does not, he thinks, have to choose between bits of things; the world cannot absorb him; he absorbs the world, his imagination never diminished by other things or beings. We should also notice that Diver's absorption process begins in historical chaos when, as Frederick Henry asserted in *A Farewell to Arms*, facts and fragments were destroying abstractions and calling in doubt the validity of all totality. Perhaps unknown to himself, Diver has covered his idealist bets with a fearful Cartesian formula: "I am others, therefore I am."

By 1929, when the boom culture in America approached collision with ungrasped realities of system, wealth for the Divers had become more and more anonymous and compulsive. "Another element that distinguished this summer and autumn for the Divers was a plenitude of money. Owing to the sale of their interest in the clinic, and to developments in America, there was now so much that the mere spending of it, the care of goods, was an absorption in itself" (276). And by April, 1930, life, internally, is ceasing to be "simply an awaiting" (275). It is as if this time of immobility parallels, psychically, the earlier meeting of two funicular cars, one descending, the other ascending the mountain. Dick, having pulled Nicole out of the abyss by his own self-gravity, has begun the sinking process and come equal with her, who is ascending, somewhere between top and bottom.

The repression of healthy desires and of a purposive, achieving manhood has given grotesque, antisocial form to Diver's needs. Greater anonymity leads to self-hatred, fear of annihilation, and, at the same time, to greater hostility toward whomever should cross his path with any comprehension of the tragedy. Nicole—this further shrinks Diver's inner margin—increasingly surfaces and articulates her concerns in a form consistent with integrity. At last she believes enough in her evolving self to accept responsibility for their lives:

> "Some of the time I think it's my fault—I've ruined you."
> "So I'm ruined, am I?" he inquired pleasantly.
> "I didn't mean that. But you used to want to create things—now you seem to want to smash them up" (286).

Nicole's words and actions flow spontaneously from her perceptions and impulses. She reacts instinctively, whereas Dick uses formulas to conceal his true feelings. As his mind creates reasons for their continued marriage, his body jerks away from Nicole's touch. Afraid of this cold withdrawal from a woman he has claimed to love with "a wild submergence of the soul" (235), Diver assumes a new mask, this time the sinister one of the confidence man:

> He covered her hand with his and said in the old pleasant voice of a conspirator for pleasure, mischief, profit, and delight:
> "See that boat out there."
> It was the motor yacht of T. F. Golding lying placid among the little swells of the Nicean bay, constantly bound upon a romantic voyage that was not dependent upon actual motion. "We'll go out there now and ask the people on board what's the matter with them" (286).

The visitation to Golding's yacht and the aimless evening's cruise illustrate the disappearance of Diver's margin of sanity held between his long-denied desires now surfacing as ugly antagonisms—demons without power—and his mask assumed for admiration's sake, his manners, charm, and seductive consideration for others. For Golding's perpetual, lush carnival extends to corrupting excess the romantic social voyages earlier captained by Dick Diver. Having been unable to escape on his own, unable now to work, unable any longer to anchor his self-indulgence to Nicole's sickness, Diver dallies for dalliance's sake. Unwilling to dive beneath his own self's facade, he will accept the *Margin* as the real world, antithetical though it is to any "actual motion" still possible in his life. Here then, the Divers' attitudes reverse; Dick seduces them both toward luxury, dissonance, a spastic dance; Nicole tries to rally Dick toward discipline, harmony, the tonic chord their life has been striving for through long periods when, often haltingly, they've practiced a regimen of the "simpler virtues." No longer can Diver blame his idleness and disintegration on Nicole. Pathetically, he even invokes Baby Warren's friendship with Golding as a reason for joining the party.

Once aboard, Nicole, the refuser, integrates into the scene; but Diver, the joiner, resists, turns isolate, and comes away humiliated because wit, timing, and grace all have failed him. In one sense Diver's garbled, fading actor's drunken performance on the *Margin* pivots on despair; seeing no one and no thing to grasp hold of, he would clear the world's deck until he regains his balance. More directly, his actions fit the framework of tantrum. Increasingly "empty-hearted" toward Nicole, Diver nevertheless had built prop by prop this socially complex world for her sake; now her health, youth, and independence ironically belittle those ten or twelve years in the creator's life. Bereft of matter from which to shape a world, Diver has nothing left but the pretense of creative detachment and impersonality.

To make matters worse, Nicole's seizing of Tommy Barban at the yacht's center stage puts Dick, who must "be admired," in the position of the missing man who is not missed. Thus his perceptions of the British clinging delusionally to the values and policies of colonialism sound like babble: ". . . It's all right for you English, you're doing a dance of death. . . . Sepoys in the ruined fort, I mean Sepoys at the gate and gaiety in the fort and all that. The green hat, the crushed hat, no future" (290). Fine; natives will overrun British colonies, and the British, with intimidating, clipped manners, will pretend for another twenty years that this fact is not so. But what of Diver's own self? His historical paradigm of reckless self-deception and vanishing empire, particularly his stumbling expression of it, turns attention to his own "ruined fort" and his dependence on critical pronouncements to avoid self-perusal. Diver has become one of those whom, like the English, he had always found antipathetic because of their subterfuges.

The unexpected appearance of Tommy Barban counterpoints Diver's self-incriminating prophecy of doom for colonialism. Still a "ruler," still a "hero," Barban opposes Diver, not simply personally, but on the political-historical level. Diver perceives the coming shifts of power in the world, but he lacks the discipline and nerve to break his servitude to an imperial system. Moreover, as a man and as a creator, "he lacks that tensile strength—none of the ruggedness of Brancusi, Leger, Picasso"; conversely, Barban, whom Fitzgerald in the same sketch called an "unbourgeoise king or nothing," [5] commits himself to exploits of action which preserve and toughen the status quo. Indeed, Diver and Barban bear some resemblance to the weakening, self-indulgent, self-deceiving Western democracies between the wars on one hand and the emerging fascist coalitions of ruthless, recessive power on the other.

Sexually, the situation's dynamics flow from Nicole's sensibility. From her viewpoint it's as if the submerged male in Diver has struggled free and come to full being in Tommy and his archetypal pursuits: "The foreignness of his depigmentation by unknown suns, his nourishment by strange soils, his tongue awkward with the curl of many dialects, his reactions attuned to odd alarms—these things fascinated and rested Nicole" (288). Wherever established aristocratic orders have been menaced, this soldier of class has kept the clock running on past time. In his very rootlessness, Barban possesses a familiarity with the regions of the earth arousing to Nicole, whose existence goes on in an enervated, artificial garden. Unlike Dick, whose maleness has been bound over to Warren husbandry only, Tommy has defined his course of action and has not been tamed by any power or any circumstances. Now, as Nicole "looked among the strangers and found, as usual, the fierce neurotics pretending calm, liking the country only in horror of the city" (289), she understandably allies with this man who has made himself briefly at home in many places and carried away the essence of each different region. Having been reassembled by a marriage that was convalescence and a convalesence that was marriage, she wants to be taken by a man who is just that—a man.

Impotent, and sensing his wife's will to be captured by Bar-

[5] Fitzgerald sketch in Mizener, *The Far Side of Paradise*, p. 348.

ban, Diver threatens to change the game and the stakes. If one compares the contingencies of life to the variables of poker, then Diver's wild card—Nicole's former absolute need to admire him —no longer has special value, but, through the dealer's whim, is simply a deuce. To dominate now, Diver's waning power must choose a final, desperate game of blackjack. Their love dead in life, Diver's will shall unite them, momentarily and for-ever, in the kingdom of death:

> "It would give me so much pleasure to think of a little some-thing I could do for you, Dick."
> He turned away from her and toward the veil of starlight over Africa.
> "I believe that's true, Nicole. And sometimes I believe that the littler it was, the more pleasure it would give you."
> "Don't talk like that."
> His face, wan in the light that the white spray caught and tossed back to the brilliant sky, had none of the lines of annoy-ance she had expected. It was even detached; his eyes focused upon her gradually as upon a chessman to be moved; in the same slow manner he caught her wrist and drew her near.
> "You ruined me, did you?" he inquired blandly. "Then we're both ruined. So—" (292).

There is a whole new world beyond them—Africa—as dark and unknown, solitary and yet divided as the veiled continent of Diver's own being. For an instant the night's beauty and splen-dor detach Diver from all the trivial and accidental colorations of his personal life. Impersonally, for a change, he hearkens back to Nicole's accusation of ruin, its pitying tones, and to his per-ception of the coming ruin of Western imperial civilizations. And Nicole, magnetized by Diver's connection with what is beyond them, even if it be death, yields to his negative force: "Cold in terror she put her other wrist into his grip. All right, she would go with him—again she felt the beauty of the night vividly in one moment of complete response and abnegation— all right, then—but now she was unexpectedly free and Dick turned his back, sighing, 'Tch! Tch!' Tears streamed down Nicole's face. In a moment she heard someone approaching; it was Tommy" (292). Out there the universe—beauty and form. In close humanity—fear and pain, a torture of complexity. Why not sever one's perception of irreconcilables through simple death?

But, having gone to the end of the line, the stern of the *Margin*, Diver cannot turn over that final ace of spades. As Nicole dares to be his, he turns away with a moral sigh, as if she had failed some subtle test of survival:

> Already with thee! tender is the night

> • • • •

> But here there is no light,
> Save what from heaven is with the breezes blown
> Through verdurous glooms and winding mossy ways.

Finally, death's night is not tender; neither from death's gorge nor from life's precipice does any light beckon. Between two worlds Diver stands, paralyzed in each, incapable of contact with either. All right then, Nicole, the woman as well as the "essence of a continent," will be taken—if we are honest about it—because of the idealist's failure of desire, taken by Barban, by the barbarian, by the plunderers, in whatever guise they come.

3

Male fortunes determined, if unfulfilled, Fitzgerald scrutinizes through Nicole and her resonance as "essence of a continent," the newest forms taken, the latest styles worn, by the body of America. Once again her private world mirrors her garden where impulses choke off words as signs of life. As before, aesthetic and sexual strains blend in common desire: "In the fine spring morning the inhibitions of the male world disappeared and she reasoned gaily as a flower, while the wind blew her hair until her head moved with it" (295). Again, the life motion of the natural elemental world awakens Nicole's vitality, this time in the daylight on a positive frequency. But back inside with Dick and Tommy she must play Sleeping Beauty still, and so express her freedom and desire only through symbolic gesture. As if to expropriate Diver's remaining identity—his role as doctor—Nicole confers upon Tommy their last bottle of camphor rub. But, Tommy gone, she lacks the confidence for any verbal showdown; repentant, "aware of the sin she had committed against him" (297), she goes upstairs to minister to the fallen Diver: "She put out her hand as if to rub his head, but he turned away like a suspicious animal. Nicole could stand the situation no longer; in a kitchen maid's panic she ran downstairs, afraid of what the stricken man above would feed on while she must continue her dry suckling at his lean chest" (297). Nicole's process of self-weaning resembles the child's; it's not so much the nourishment as the form of contact which reassures her that the world will be the same after her separation.

Rosemary's return soon substitutes gall for Diver's psychological milk. Now Nicole goes to the beach brittley resistant and "with a renewal of her apprehension that Dick was contriving at some desperate solution" (298). Unlike five years ago, hysteria is no longer a possible response for her. If her league with Tommy on the *Margin* and at the Villa Diana the morning after indicated her simple desire for a stronger man, then the beach episode spurs Nicole to analytical judgment. To choose Tommy externally, she must see Dick annihilated in that sphere of life which decides among persons and relationships. For Nicole reality is material and physical, its moral coordinate property; therefore Diver must be a verifiable ruin, physically as well as psychologically, if, in fact, he is to disappear from her field of reality.

Nicole, herself, awaits not any gradual, organic metamorphosis, but a transformation closer in speed and composition to those rapid elemental changes in chemistry. Fitzgerald associates her leap into new being with the machine and the aesthetic of power and dominion for which it stands in America: "Nicole had been *designed* for change, for flight, with money as fins and wings. The new state of things would be no more than if a *racing chassis*, concealed for years under the body of a *family limousine*, should be stripped to its original self" (298, my italics). Whatever the medium, competitive desire and capacity underlie whatever graceful guise appears to contain such raw power. In Fitzgerald's vision personality has abdicated the creative imperative given it by Hart Crane when he wrote that "unless poetry can absorb the machine, i.e., acclimatize it as naturally and casually as trees, cattle, galleons, castles and all other human associations of the past, then poetry has failed of its full contemporary function." [6] But it is the machine which has captured and absorbed personality. To Crane one must respond that in America the aesthetic impulse toward natural and cultural objects has always fought unsuccessfully against aggressive drives. It is logical that a society which conquered nature with machines would, in its own body, be mechanized by the same drives in abstract form. Nicole Warren's leap will not be any romantic, humanist flight into more sympathetic and imaginative consciousness. Unlike complex Icarus, who designed both confining labyrinth and liberating wings, Nicole *has been designed*. An artifact of her inheritance, she will be propelled by the energy of dynastic money, of a civilization's system. The limousine and its connotations of class, elegance, and beauty are but concessions to form, euphemisms which legitimize and strengthen rigidities of class and power.

When he designates money as fuel for the machine, Fitzgerald alludes to the dimension of place and personality. Or, as his middle-class figure in "The Swimmers" said: "Americans should be born with fins, and perhaps they were—perhaps

---

[6] Hart Crane, *The Collected Poems*, ed. and intro. by Waldo Frank (New York: Liveright, 1946), p. 177.

money was a form of fin. In England, property begot a strong place sense, but Americans, restless and with shallow roots, needed fins and wings." [7] Allied to the rootless machine, money will forge such mechanical fins and wings. The automobile, quickly mass-produced, articulated American restlessness and movement among many places without respect or contact. Nicole Warren's technologically created self should be compared to a "racing chassis," for as a wanderer, an exile, a lady of many places, not one of them known by her, she will race from place to beautiful place seeking proprietary rights, while true destination eludes her and her new chauffeur, Barban, the daredevil driver.

As always, Fitzgerald does not permit metaphor to drown out the voice of Nicole's personality: "Nicole could feel the fresh breeze already—it was the wrench she feared, and the dark manner of its coming" (298). Her birth will be neither so simple nor so clean as a chassis rolling off one of Henry Ford's assembly lines. For the purpose of Nicole's metamorphosis, the Adam and Eve birth myth seems to reverse its male-female values of independence and dependence. In the beginning as *Genesis* told it and as it operated within Dick Diver, the male dreamed his Eve and woke to find the form of his image embodied in the substance of his own flesh. Psychologically, Nicole came of Diver; she existed for him in fantasy before she ever appeared in his world. Now, however, Nicole seems unable to come to new and separate birth until Diver goes to sleep again, but a sleep of nightmare, not of dream. "The wrench she feared" is herself psychologically breaking from Diver's side, and "the dark manner of its coming" can mean only the dissolution of the parent self, of Dick's self, intact yet incomplete without her, and cut off from contact with woman and with everything else in the world. It's as if to stay in Eden means death and that, in the modern America of this novel, only woman will take her

---

[7] F. Scott Fitzgerald, in notes to *Tender Is the Night* in *Three Novels* (New York: Charles Scribner's Sons, 1953), p. 355.

chances in the fallen world of history and society. The man will sleep until death parts him from his dreams. But in this context, the dream itself and its idealizing mode of perception, rather than Eve, destroys Adam. Or, as Fitzgerald described the transfer of vitality from Dick to Nicole: "It seems as if the completion of his ruination will be the fact that cures her— almost mystically." [8] Dick may have mastered the paternal role, but Nicole has had too many fathers; to be whole, she must break the pattern.

Just as Fitzgerald renders Nicole as an industrial object which pulls its weight in the total system, Nicole begins to see Diver less as man and more as thing. Her choice of object too relegates Diver to an undynamic, past context, one very different from her own. "His old expertness with people," she compares to a "tarnished object of art" (300). Sensing this and down to the nub of himself, Diver goes to physical accomplishment, a "lifting trick" expressive of stamina and timing. Performed for Rosemary, a stranger to his actual condition, Diver's exhibition becomes a psychological artifice as well. But, these acrobatics having failed humiliatingly, what seems to separate Nicole most utterly from Diver is his own mere detachment. "Expressionless, alone with the water and the sky" (303), his mask belittles Nicole's pity and, worse than that, her straining with him as he had tried to lift the man on his shoulders. His silent, arrogant disclaimer of actions, which, moments before, he had put body and soul into accomplishing, must drive off any love or sympathy. As the idealist gathered others around him in success, the skeptic must bear the conditions of human failure alone. It is a false dignity. Unable to love, Diver cannot come out of himself to allow anyone else to love or even touch him.

Back on the beach, with Rosemary for catalyst, Diver tries to codify the relationship between roles and personality. " 'The danger to an actress is in responding' " (306); and responding, it develops, consists of externalizing one's genuine emotions in

[8] Fitzgerald sketch in Mizener, *The Far Side of Paradise*, p. 352.

a trying situation. The difficulty, given the egocentric necessity of an actress, is that spontaneity focuses the audience's attention on whatever is objective in the situation, instead of on the actress. According to Diver, Rosemary, or anyone, must " 'do the unexpected thing until you've maneuvered the audience back from the objective fact to yourself' " (306). On stage and— since the dramatic metaphor has tutored personality in this novel—in life, one's best human self is expendable. Individuality depends upon one's capacity to deny contingency and to substitute an unexpected and unfelt gesture for the " 'correct emotional responses—fear and love and sympathy' " (306). This theory accepted, any spontaneity would come from the head, from faculties of calculation rather than from the heart and its sources of sympathy. Addressed to Rosemary, Diver's advice has some pertinence, for, individually, she lacks both an emotional and a perceptual life. Only the tricks of the trade can rescue her from mediocrity. Diver, however, if he is to ease his own malaise, must follow T. S. Eliot's advice and use form as a means of escape from passion and personality.[9]

For, to preserve an identity worthy of center stage, Diver has molded his role and gestures out of a self less and less capable of responding with anything but bitterness. Time and time again, he has blunted Nicole's critical perception of one or another of his outrages by substituting detachment for spontaneous emotional response. Nicole thus wonders about his whereabouts of consciousness and forgets the annoying "objective fact." The dramatic situation enclosing Diver while he speaks illustrates the limitation of his paradigm. With his "unexpected" lecture, he has stolen center stage from gullible Rosemary, but there is no longer enough there to hold Nicole's attention. For her, the elaborateness of the ploy spells his desperation. But perhaps Nicole's abrupt departure is what Dick desires; one no longer knows his motives, nor does one have faith in their conse-

[9] T. S. Eliot, "Tradition and the Individual Talent," *The Sacred Wood* (London: Methuen, 1920).

quences. As actor-director, he is no longer interesting; his mode has become more abstract than dramatic.

Her ego stymied in the labyrinth, Nicole will not seek a forward path; instead she retraces her steps and escapes back at the starting point of the Warren past. Lost in Diver's world of euphemism and, now, annihilation, she'll reject sensibility and tenderness and do what a healthy, intact Warren would have done in the beginning: marry a man of power, Tommy Barban, a twentieth-century barbarian of the old order. Fed up with those places "where she had played planet to Dick's sun" (307), Nicole does not rebel against male authority in itself; what seems intolerable is that Dick's "sun" shines with gaslight upon the twentieth century. Long ago her broken self had given over the thinking to him, but Diver's mind yielded to the denial of reality through genteel affectations: "It had been a long lesson but she had learned it. Either you think—or else others have to think for you and take power from you, pervert and discipline your natural tastes, civilize and sterilize you" (308). Her defensive, either-or rhetoric, strikingly close to that of dispossessed minorities, tenaciously reinforces Warren opposition to any diminution of their power. Diver's values were blown to bits in the trenches, and the rubble cannot camouflage Nicole's unsatisfied female needs.

Through all of Nicole's changes, Diver continues to act like a man condemned to replay forever one of the games in *Alice in Wonderland*.

> 'Thank y' father-r
> Thank y' mother-r
> Thanks for meeting up with one another—"

"I don't like that one," Dick said, starting to turn the page (308). Forced to deal with submerged reality, Diver's instincts go back to the nineteenth century; his reflex belongs not so much to the psychiatrist and husband who must recognize a woman's strength and possibilities as it does to the Victorian gentleman, perhaps to his clergyman father who thought that, if ignored long enough, nasty facts would go away. Dick too retreats, but not to those spare-bodied men of early Virginia or to that ancestral power represented by Mad Anthony Wayne and the great-grandfather who was governor of North Carolina. For form's sake Diver returns to the highly conscious good manners learned early from his father and manners which served that clergyman well in Gilded Age drawing rooms at ladies' teas. Such affected social graces may have determined the young Southerner's survival in the North at that period, but they are, in the twentieth century, a substitute for life and vitality, and only that. Whatever their effect upon women initially, these manners emasculate the men who wear them, make them first gentle men, and then boys. Nicole, partly because of Dick's failure, looks to the past for a tradition of mere strength and ruthlessness, while Diver seeks to rationalize weakness and incapacity. Both find what they seek—parallel histories that cannot meet without conquest and absorption.

Like Pallas Athene with whom she earlier allied herself, Nicole Warren leaves little to chance. As she prepares for Tommy Barban, whom she has summoned, she sees herself more as capital property—in all its changing guises—than as woman: "She bathed and anointed herself and covered her body with a layer of powder, while her toes crunched another pile on a bath towel. She looked microscopically at the lines of her flanks, wondering how soon the fine, slim edifice would begin to sink squat and earthward" (309). Simultaneously, she is filly and horse-trader, herself with female desires and Sid Warren, profiteer. How much am I worth? she inquires, while bathing and anointing abdicate their religious and sexual purpose for a fertility of capital value. Subtly, the metaphorical object evolves from horse to edifice with its suggestion of the great American skyscrapers, those houses of monopoly power for the expanding American empire. Clearly, Fitzgerald is transforming Nicole as "essence of a continent" into twentieth-century America, for in the nineteenth century the country's resources were natural things. Then, the land and its inhabitants—horses and humans —were traded. Now, in 1930, the character of the nation shows in its architectural face. Skyscrapers shelter an increasingly bureaucratic and abstract system, so that Fitzgerald's choice of edifice contrasts with Hart Crane's vision of modern technology (the Brooklyn Bridge) as a span between body and consciousness, between the remote spaces of a disunified continent. Because he compares woman, not man, to edifice, Fitzgerald recalls Paul Rosenfeld's description of the American leisure woman as a "magnificently shining edifice." "Flowing of line and rich in material, it has also made of her a dwelling uninhabited, gray, chill like the houses where the furniture stands year-long in twilight under its shrouds. For, in keeping the male undeveloped and infantile, American culture has attributed the masculine principle to the female, and divided the female against her proper intuitions." [10]

As Nicole derives her historical image first from natural and then from architectural phenomena, so her psychological self-impression is inculcated by Hollywood, that funneler of dreams to every citizen without differentiation among rich and poor. In *Tender Is the Night* the women become Daddy's Girls one way or another: Baby Warren, the unattached, androgynous object who has superimposed a Robber Baron consciousness upon her female body; Rosemary Hoyt, who, on the screen, lures the world away from realities of time and history, and, in life, lures men away from maturity. Finally, Nicole too surrenders what is of value in herself—"the essential structure and economy," the "promise" of a "true growing" (33)—for Rosemary's notion of youth as power. It's as if loss of innocence means the end rather than the beginning of one's fulfillment. For maturity involves personality with dissipation and death. Adult perception carries

[10] Paul Rosenfeld, *Port of New York* (Urbana: University of Illinois Press, 1961), pp. 209–10.

with it the conviction, always agonizingly felt, of life's unalterable necessities; whereas innocence cultivates a sense of invulnerability, imperviousness, and imperishability. Perhaps one reason women cannot grow up is that the men who determine mass culture in America are psychological boys who require younger sisters for mates. In any case, Nicole Warren's particular desire "to be worshipped again, to pretend to have a *mystery*," follows from her consciousness of loss, because of her illness, of "two of the great arrogant years in the life of a pretty girl" (309, my italics). Thus, for Nicole and perhaps for America, the lust for false youth is itself a fearful, immature response to the ravishing of girl and of continent when each was genuinely young and uncontaminated.

In Nicole's encounter with Barban, an opposition between natural and civilized states occurs once more. But when he asks her, " 'Why didn't they leave you in your natural state?' " he's talking about a condition of personality where action is beyond morality, not about any Edenic state where innocence and spontaneity are themselves values and ways of being. He is referring to Nicole's power to pick and choose among the world's best: " 'I'm just a whole lot of simple people,' " she tells him. Clearly, this collection of persons depends more upon her imperial, dynastic context than it does upon any condition of innocence. For her, freedom from the usual psychic bankruptcy, after the losses inflicted by violation, flows from her money. No matter what tremors may shake exposed buildings, this American edifice, girded by money, property, and connections, will remain an intact skeleton. Whatever quivers do get through will affect only the surfaces of self and society.

Assessing her "white crook's eyes" as she and Barban ride to Nice, Nicole concludes decisively: "Very well then, better a sane crook than a mad puritan' " (312). This utter paucity of alternatives terribly indicts the American condition. We have watched the puritan madness paralyze Dick Diver because, in his idealist self-worship, he first identified himself as elite and elect and then believed in his power to determine the election of others. Himself having become implicated in complexities of desire and guilt, he could not face the world but clung, in his mind, to images of innocence and beauty. At last he hates himself and the world because of realities he did not acknowledge before the ideal vision became bindingly fixed. In the face of reality's contingencies and necessities, puritan ideal and moral absolutes turn one away from life and history toward an isolate, martyr's existence—an asceticism from compulsion, in a body which has dried up. No question should be raised over Nicole's rejection of this deathbound way of seeing and living. But what of "sane crook"? Why are "sane" and "crook" linked? What conception of personality necessarily emerges? Clearly, this paradigm confirms the social Darwinist conception of society and the individual. For sanity will consist of, and be verified by, survival. And one survives through seizure and mastery, by that violent predatory cycle of strong and weak which governs the life process and metes out death and extinction to creatures and species unable to cope with and adapt to the changing conditions of this perpetual struggle. In America, the materialist forces were able, as well or better than the idealists, to build an empire on the rock of elect doctrine. Always concerned with evidence, demonstration, and proof, a materialist would demand earthly evidence of any individual's privilege. For them election meant wealth, and wealth requires power.

The limitation of Nicole's "sane crook" prescription is that it denies a certain rich part of her nature and of human personality in general. Neither does it deal with the demonic turn often taken when sensibility and tenderness are trampled within a person. If her paradigm is accepted in society and among societies, then Spengler's prophecy of "gang rule," of "the world as spoil" to be taken by the most brutal and cunning plunderers will come true—as, in fact, it was realized by the Fascist coalitions and as it is currently realized by American and Soviet empires.[11] Since sanity depends upon theft and force, what happens when America, or that new world of Africa, is stolen and ravished entirely? Ultimately, the prey disappear, and the sane crooks must fight each other. Given its own logic and given the world crisis of human and natural resources, pragmatism alone calls for the rejection of Nicole's chosen alternative. If the integrity of others is not perceived and respected in action, on what psychological foundation will identity rest except that of murder? What Jonathan Edwards, that idealist of humane method and sensibility, two hundred years ago called "benevolence" (disinterested affection) toward other beings seems in twentieth-century America an absolute qualification for sanity and survival.

So much for the hope of a new world, a reconstructed social and economic order in America. What the Warren-Barban alliance prophesies is the reformation and revitalization of America's imperial power. In this connection D. H. Lawrence's analysis of the emerging historical situation offers a vision truer and more terrible than Spengler's prophecy of a worsening cycle of dynamic, barbaric, anarchic civilization:

> For there are not now, as in the Roman times, any great reservoirs of energetic barbaric life. Goths, Gauls, Germans, Slavs, Tartars. The world is very full of people, but all fixed in civilizations of their own, and they have all our vices, all our mechanisms, and all our means of destruction. This time, the leading civilization cannot die out as Greece, Rome, Persia died. It must suffer a great collapse, maybe. But it must carry through all the collapse the living clue to the next civilization.[12]

Unlike Spengler's notion of the earth ruled and patrolled by its dregs, Lawrence's categorical prophecy assumes that no matter how ragged the coat of civilization, certain threads are woven in

[11] This cultural prophecy of Spengler's made a powerful impression on Fitzgerald's sense of history. See Turnbull, ed., *Letters of F. Scott Fitzgerald*, p. 290.
[12] D. H. Lawrence, *Psychoanalysis and the Unconscious and Fantasia of the Unconscious* (New York: Viking Press, 1960), p. 208.

continuity. If we try out Lawrence's imperative on the metallic evolutions strengthened by the merger of Barban and Warren, we must conclude that Fitzgerald does not look for the collapse, cyclic or linear, of America's capitalist industrial empire. Rather, he proposes the additional consolidation of power and wealth through Tommy Barban's authority and courage, with Barban the representative of a new elite—cultured, reactionary, nihilist leaders.

To set in motion the latest phase in American aristocratic-barbarian civilization, Fitzgerald brings Tommy and Nicole to Beaulieu, easternmost spot on the French Riviera. "Symbolically she lay across his saddle-bow as surely as if he had wolfed her away from Damascus and they had come out upon the Mongolian plain" (316). The echo of hoof-beats conjures up North African slave markets and girls bought and stolen away to tribal destinations across the steppes to Mongolia, with all its memories of Genghis Khan, who terrorized and exploited Europe as its later civilized-barbaric conquerors would America, Africa, and Asia. Here Nicole gladly surrenders herself—woman, property, and continent—to Barban's displaced, anti-personal male authority.

Imperceptibly yet totally, she rejects Diver's values and their genteel codification as a system of interlocked manners and morals: "Moment by moment all that Dick had taught her fell away and she was ever nearer to what she had been in the beginning, prototype of that obscure yielding up of swords that was going on in the world about her. Tangled with love in the moonlight she welcomed the anarchy of her lover" (316). Whose swords? What surrender? Prototype Nicole certainly is. Fulfilled by her new union, this barbarian aristocracy opposes the genuine sensibility of some eighteenth- and early nineteenth-century European and American families who, often because of roots in what Yeats romantically called "one dear perpetual place," brought to their exercise of power and authority a degree

of loveliness, custom, ceremony, and aesthetic grace.[13] The Warrens, now the Barbans, represent an aristocracy reconstructed
along feudal principles, whose muscle does not derive from
continuity, originality, or sensibility, but from simple money,
complex property, and the centrifugal power these things confer
in a modern imperial system. One should not be misled by the
allusion to anarchy. For anarchy, as fascism so well showed, can
be both catalyst and instrument for the totalitarian exercise of
political power. Likewise, at this time, political fascism signaled
an abandonment of the attempt to evolve genuine democracies
from republics whose original base and intent were elitist in
nature. Now Barban may be anarchic to fulfill his desires and to
become one of the new rulers, but he is not anarchic in any
political, economic, or philosophic sense. Rather, he would impose ruthless punishment upon any who opposed consolidation
of personal fortunes within national and supra-national empires.
Moreover his merger with Nicole symbolically parallels the gut
alliances of fascism. The industrial Warrens in coalition with
the militarist Barban form a cartel eager for spoils, with all the
world their prey.

4

Back at the Villa Diana, stripped of mystery and
spontaneity with Tommy, Nicole pauses to consider the un-
spoken depths of her tie to Dick. Here, at the last, Diver's body
directs and acts for his being. There exists no more stage, no
props; in their absence, gestures flow unconsidered, unimpeded,
unexpurgated from deepest consciousness. When Dick does not
answer her accusations of cowardice and failure, Nicole shakily
begins "to feel the old hypnotism of his intelligence, sometimes
exercised without power but always with substrata of truth under

---

[13] W. B. Yeats, "A Prayer for My Daughter," *The Collected Poems of
W. B. Yeats* (New York: Macmillan, 1956), p. 186.

truth which she could not break or even crack" (310). In its silent intimidation, Diver's intelligence conceals a confused and paralyzed self which now chooses to be mired in complexities in order to rationalize away realities of desire and history. Neither personality nor history stands still; whether motion be forward or backward, constructive or entropic, there will be motion and change. Unfortunately, when Nicole rejects Diver's euphemism and gentility, she scorns as well genuine values of personality—benevolence, consideration, and tolerance. Although Diver's nostalgic humanism comes to mask viciousness, at his best he did recognize aesthetic form and humane sensibility as essential to a richly developed nature. Before his own self split apart, there was in Diver, as there seems always to be in Fitzgerald's sympathetic complexity, a commitment to warmth and tenderness as qualities upon which civilized men and societies must stand. Nicole's transferral to Barban ends the search for personality and for a true and complex relatedness. The few flowing lines of the limousine have been scrapped and melted back to ore; all that remains is the chassis, the machine itself.

At liberty now from Nicole, Dr. Diver is not liberated from the motivations, the vision, and the inner weakness which patterned his life. To make this absolutely clear, Fitzgerald invents an episode in which Diver, against his own common sense, goes into verbal conflict as the leisure-class knight. This time far from being at its "truly most brilliant and glamorous," the leisure class exhibits only perversity and squalor.[14] In any case the knight's ordeal consists of freeing from prison Mary North Minghetti and Lady Caroline Sibley-Biers who have been jailed as a result of their sexual duplicity. Diver, the rescuer, possesses no magic with which to lift the curse of sterility. All he does, in mythic terms, is release the sick women into the world to further pollute the wasteland: "He would have to go fix this thing that he didn't care a damn about, because it had early

[14] Fitzgerald sketch in Mizener, *The Far Side of Paradise*, p. 346.

become a habit to be loved, perhaps from the moment when he had realized that he was the last hope of a dying clan" (321). Now the "last hope" of this or any other "dying clan" does have choices. He can forget the clan, or, if he will pick and choose among its values, he can extend the best of past traditions to different persons whose own vitality and history might create a richer, more integrated clan suitable for the changed conditions of the present. Or, lacking confidence and fearful of failure, he can become the servant of that establishment which has put out of business his own and many another clan. Finally, his servant's cry of "Use me!" translates self-doubt and uncertainty about his place in the scheme of things into a plea for approval by those who own the mansion.

Ben Franklin, Horatio Alger, Booker T. Washington, S. I. Hayakawa—success for those who start as outsiders in America ultimately depends upon whether their rise involves incorporation into the American establishment. This need to belong, to be legitimate, to be approved and admired, has its origins in the failure of roots in America, a failure of lineage. In a passage from "The Swimmers," later distilled into the *Notebooks*, Fitzgerald talks about the process through which abstract illusion and material power distort and betray the impulse to serve America democratically: "France was a land, England was a people, but America, having about it still that quality of the idea, was harder to utter—it was the graves at Shiloh and the tired, drawn, nervous faces of its great men, and the country boys dying in the Argonne for a phrase that was empty before their bodies withered. It was a willingness of the heart." [15] Clearly, one must distinguish between the poor "country boys dying in the Argonne" and Richard Diver, lured by his middle-class educational deferment to delusions of privilege in Vienna. Both respond to the bait of empty phrases, but there is a pathos about the dead boys' innocence of American empire—an excuse,

[15] Fitzgerald, *The Crack-Up*, p. 197.

whereas Diver's idealist complicity is less "a willingness of the heart" than a willingness to risk identity, integrity, and independence on behalf of his own American future.

Given the facts of American history—its great building blocks of genocide, slavery, plunder of a continent—and its outrageous self-justifications, innocence as a point of view has become a national crime. About those lost American dead, Fitzgerald shows a considerate respect. Moved by their "willingness of the heart," their intuitive commitment to other human beings, he merely elegizes them because in American history there seems little opportunity to tie that willingness to integrity and reality through national structures. His heart "determined to make them otherwise," Fitzgerald's intelligence sees and records the likelihood that, in America, "things are hopeless." [16]

Rescuing the two decadent women, Diver uses wit and parody to spare himself humiliation as well as to serve his masters well. Yet his parody of American and British fortune and nobility reinforces the very realities it would undermine. Still present in Diver beneath the irony is a hint of the pride defined by David Halberstam in his trenchant essay on McGeorge Bundy: "He believed if *he* set *his mind* to it there was nothing *American power* couldn't do." [17] The fact is that Diver's garbled and highly ironic allusions to John D. Rockefeller, Mellon, and Lord Henry Ford do free the women, exactly because these are not fictitious names in a vacuum but the great realities behind American power. In *Tender Is the Night*'s vision of the actual America, there is no vessel for that "willingness of the heart" so essential to the creation of a history that will dignify individual personality.

It remains, through confrontation with Barban with Nicole as booty and witness, for Fitzgerald to finish off Diver even as a will. In an important way neither Dick nor Tommy is central

[16] *Ibid.*, p. 69.
[17] David Halberstam, "The Very Expensive Education of McGeorge Bundy," *Harper's*, vol. 239 (July, 1969), p. 32. My italics.

here; the exchange relies upon Nicole as conductor of energy, "so that their emotions pass through her divided self as through a bad telephone connection" (327). Once more Fitzgerald locates Nicole's reference point in a metallic object, an instrument which scientifically, mechanically, automatically, registers and also distorts the complexities of human voices, desires, and personalities. In the conversation Diver parries into absurdity Tommy's rational, logical case for divorce. At last, when Tommy impatiently switches to impulse, Diver withdraws matter of factly, as if his abdication depended not upon any involvement or any passion but simply upon the appropriate mode of perception:

> "That is so useless. Nicole and I love each other, that's all there is to it."
> "Well then," said the Doctor, "since it's all settled, suppose we go back to the barber shop" (329).

Fitzgerald's rare use of "the Doctor" suggests an impersonal case. No longer lover or husband, Diver thinks to preserve his dignity by washing his hands in the most careful fashion. Such meticulousness has nothing to do with the patient or the wife, but signifies all that is left of Diver—a mere persona of professional form.

Suddenly and from nowhere another world comes into being. Circles of reality widen from the Tour de France or from Diver's table, whichever one chooses as the arbitrary starting point:

> First was a lone cyclist in a red jersey, toiling intent and confident out of the westering sun, passing to the melody of a high chattering cheer. Then three together in a harlequinade of faded color, legs caked yellow with dust and sweat, faces expressionless, eyes heavy and endlessly tired.
> Tommy faced Dick, saying: "I think Nicole wants a divorce— I suppose you'll make no obstacles?"
> A troupe of fifty more swarmed after the first bicycle racers, strung out over two hundred yards; a few were smiling and

self-conscious, a few obviously exhausted, most of them in-
different and weary. A retinue of small boys passed, a few defiant
stragglers, a light truck carried the victims of accident and
defeat (328–29).

This impersonal trail of life sobers even Barban into a qualified
courtesy. From the race there is no exile; even its victims are
borne along the course in a truck, a mockery of past effort, past
vitality. Aesthetically, the bicycle race is exactly that—a bicycle
race; no symbol, no allusion, no moralism arrives to assign it an
ordered place. The sheerly perceptual modality corresponds to
that anonymous relationship experienced by Tommy and Nicole
in their order of personality. Although there might be clear
analogy between Diver's passage out of life and the decrepitude
of the cyclers, the connection does not reach us in any simply
equivalent way. Achieved here is the aesthetic of "magic sugges-
tiveness" [18] which Joseph Conrad and Edmund Wilson, in essays
mulled over by Fitzgerald, both related to music, "the art of
arts." "One of the principal aims of symbolism," Wilson wrote,
"was to approximate the indefiniteness of music." [19] Indeed, the
scene ends with the music of film. As Diver fades out through
widening circles of reality, Nicole's eyes simulate a camera until
with a vanishing poof his existence ceases to be verified. At this
point, Nicole's perception has less freedom and range than a
camera's. Her mobility riveted by other circumstances, her eyes,
at least in relation to Diver's movements, are not moving but
stationary.

Fittingly, Fitzgerald renders the last scenario from the beach
Diver built in a triple perspective which fulfills the form and
prophecy of Rosemary's Angle: that of Nicole and her compan-
ions, that of Dick, and that of the event itself, impersonal and
without moral or historical interpretative structure. Allusion and
reflection have receded before fact and event. Tempted to direct

[18] Joseph Conrad, "Preface," The Nigger of the Narcissus (New York:
Doubleday, Page, 1924), p. xiii.
[19] Edmund Wilson, as quoted by Sheilah Graham in College of One (New
York: Bantam Books, 1968), p. 110.

a last drama, Diver creates, with intellect and no imagination, a world empty save for himself and Mary Minghetti. Diver's manufactured desire desperately asserts mind over matter in order to stave off the unalterable circumstances of his context. His synthetic drama seems an act geared to nothing but himself and, even there, geared only to the masturbation of his ego. Now an idealist confidence man, Diver does not for a moment entertain for himself the illusion he would make real to Mary. But, with a sudden lens change, Fitzgerald clarifies Diver's motive: "His eyes, for the moment clear as a child's asked her sympathy and stealing over him he felt the old necessity of convincing her that he was the last man in the world and she was the last woman. . . . Then he would not have to look at those other figures, a man and a woman, black and white and metallic against the sky . . ." (332). In this inorganic, imperial garden, Tommy and Nicole are Adam and Eve. Leisured, self-sufficient, metallic creations, they are sustained in their garden by the system which exploits and dehumanizes the world. Fiercely brittle, they lack all hope of fluidity, depth, and richness of being. For these twentieth-century historical archetypes, creation has consisted of metamorphosis not from the earth's slime but from the inorganic mind of the machine. Like computers, what is most formidable about them is the stark fact of their existence.

Against this reality, the plastic world Diver conjures up silently with Mary, and which she grasps at, disappears first in his mind and then from their movable stage: "His glance fell soft and kind upon hers, suggesting an emotion underneath; their glances married suddenly, bedded, strained together. Then, as the laughter inside him became so loud that it seemed as if Mary must hear it, Dick switched off the light and they were back in the Riviera sun" (333). Here drama and gesture do not extend consciousness but create a facade for unrevealed perceptions. Diver's interior laughter—in the neurotic, laughter serves isolation instead of community—recalls his faculty of detachment, yet in the past that quality worked on behalf of engagement rather than abdication. Diver's fantasies of sexuality utterly protect and prevent him from any sensuous contact. His intelligence feeds only on its own shrinking carcass.

Whatever actions Diver performs open up alternatives to others only. Even his last gesture, a papal cross of renunciation, seems calculated to inspire motion toward him by Nicole, but she has surrendered her remaining freedom to Barban: " 'I'm going to him,' Nicole got to her knees. 'No, you're not,' said Tommy, pulling her down firmly. 'Let well enough alone' " (333). This moment signifies the final conquest. Her simple and separate impulse is repelled by virtue of his physical force. Tommy lives and has prospered in a monolithic world, and therefore he will permit no complexity or diversity of response, even if such an action involves no division of allegiance. "Let well enough alone" means Barban intends to shut the gates of his garden against the world until all antithetical creatures are exiled or extinct.

5

The brief coda to *Tender Is the Night* reverberates themes, pans time and space, and blacks out those perspectives through which Fitzgerald had been rendering Diver's loss of self and history. We cease to see Diver, either directly or through anyone else's eyes, whether character or novelist; all we have about him is second-hand information—letters from him to Nicole and, finally, bits of gossip that filter back to her. Facts, what few facts there are, grow less and less graspable; suppositions replace facts, and assumption becomes commensurate with truth.

Like America's original natives, Diver wanders from place to place until he loses name, identity, and connection with other persons, other things, other times and places. From postmarks Nicole traces him to Geneva, New York, a long journey from that other Geneva whose cultural vision has haunted Diver to extinction. Now there is no cultural center and no anarchy either, for the Warren-Barban cartel prospers greatly even in the face of world depression. But history must be satisfied with Nicole's vague memory. All flesh scraped away, Fitzgerald's ending appears with taut aesthetic perfection: "She looked up Geneva in an atlas and found it was in the heart of the Finger Lakes section and considered a pleasant place. Perhaps, so she liked to think, his career was biding its time, again like Grant's in Galena; his latest note was post-marked from Hornell, New York, which is some distance from Geneva and a very small town; in any case he is almost certainly in that section of the country, in one town or another" (334). Nicole Warren, contemporary national goddess, has to discover America through an atlas. Could it be there is a place untouched, a "section of the country" unsectioned by the centuries of exploration? From Nicole we'll never know. Letter gives way to note, and note to guess; Buffalo—for man and for beast the name of American history is annihilation—yields to a succession of small towns which fade to "a very small town." Diver's journey, its purpose, duration, and destination, all are distilled by the indefinite, uncaring "some."

About history Nicole is as ignorant as she is of geography. For U. S. Grant's last return to Galena, Illinois, was a biding of time until death. Then, in the 1880's after he had presided, half unwittingly, over Reconstruction along monopolist, racist lines, Grant went back to Galena to write his *Personal Memoirs* and to die, in his own mind absolved from complicity in America's degradation. With a vicious sentimentality, he refers in the final pages of the *Memoirs* to the Civil War as if no history had intervened between it and the present: "The war has made us a nation of great power and intelligence. We have but little to do to preserve peace, happiness, and prosperity at home, and the respect of other nations. Our experience ought to teach us the necessity of the first; our power secures the latter. I feel that we are on the eve of a new era, when there is to be great harmony between the Federal and Confederate. I cannot stay to be a living witness to the correctness of this prophecy; but I feel it within me that it is to be so." [20] When judgment becomes thus rationalized to prophecy, how fitting it is for Fitzgerald, at the last, to say nothing about history. Diver, unlike Grant, has no last words of encouragement or bitterness, but his talents have been destroyed by the same forces of innocence and idealism within, and aggrandizement without, which rendered Grant historically senile. As personal historian, Nicole resembles Grant. How American it is to remember with sentimental conviction whatever it is we have degraded.

Although, because vague, Nicole's casual tones would make everything well, the unassuming camera through dissolving general shots follows Diver farther and farther from any center of human consciousness. Diver and the America he could not discover because he would not accept its reality are too blurred to be observed in a closeup. At the end of *The Waste Land*, T. S. Eliot offers his personae and his audience fragments to "shore up against [their] ruins," but in *Tender Is the Night* form provides no such alternative. On the contrary, here form has extinguished its own light for the journey into darkness. For Diver and for America the night will not be tender—not in any case or any aspect:

> We were the last romantics—chose for theme
> Traditional sanctity and loveliness;
> Whatever's written in what poets name
> The book of the people; whatever most can bless
> The mind of man or elevate a rhyme;
> But all is changed, that high horse riderless,
> Though mounted in that saddle Homer rode
> Where the swan drifts upon a darkening flood.[21]

[20] *Personal Memoirs of U. S. Grant* (New York: Charles L. Webster, 1886), vol. 2, p. 553.
[21] Yeats, "Coole Park and Ballylee, 1931," *Collected Poems*, p. 240.

To even survive, Fitzgerald's form implies, we must leave Dick Diver in some forgotten place, leave him there like that other lost dreamer, Rip Van Winkle, sleeping the oblivious sleep of the dead.

PART III

nine

The fall to earth

1

Artifice, as the mythical Daedalus could not teach his son Icarus, is only a gambit. Beyond the categories of intellect and imagination, and beyond the category of man, the external conditions of life impose necessity upon all human beings. Whatever an individual's genius, effort, and will, circumstances can strike him down for no reason and according to no pattern that he can see. In the case of F. Scott Fitzgerald fate seems to have timed its final blow in inverse proportion to his deserts. For after he recognized an inevitability, a justice, and a process in his psychic and aesthetic crack-up following *Tender Is the Night,* he remained faithful enough to life and to his craft to reassemble the pieces and make another start. The loose ends justify that commitment and that effort. However tentative, fragmentary, and merely suggestive his aesthetic remains, their vessel, *The Last Tycoon,* maintains its stature as an accomplishment on behalf of American society. Indeed, the unfinished nature of *The Last Tycoon* may disorient and jar us into awareness of the unnatural incompletion afflicting our American identity.

Able to function again, Fitzgerald did not evade and flee the present to seek a lost and largely imaginary past. On the contrary, he went back to Hollywood in July, 1937, to fulfill his responsibilities to Zelda, now permanently gone from him, and to his daughter; but he moved west also to establish an independent attitude toward the past so that he could, when the opportunity presented itself, live and write in a new context. That his life abruptly ended before *The Last Tycoon* matured to final form does not change that novel's inconclusiveness. Yet even as a work-in-progress *The Last Tycoon* does document Fitzgerald's tougher pragmatic and even phenomenological stance toward history and personality and toward the novel's relationship to life, generally and in an American context of business and technology.

Certainly, Fitzgerald's mutations of subject and theme are considerable. For his central figure he chose Monroe Stahr, whose Jewish immigrant background immunized him from Jay Gatsby's unthinking, sheerly desirous idealism and from Dick Diver's paralyzing, middle-class "good instincts." In a further innovation Fitzgerald locates Stahr in the milieu of American industry as the executive who knows where everything is, who unifies production through will and grasp of contingencies. Essential to this character's relevance and complexity is Fitzgerald's shift in intellectual context from idealist to rationalist. He conceives of Stahr as one who had early considered the world with an outsider's eyes and instinctively decided " 'this is all wrong— a mess—all a lie—and a sham.' " [1] Stahr then extended the Cartesian proof of existence into a method of creative dominion in his society's business and cultural life. If existence derives from thought and perception, so should power and creation; if, given the proper formula, the mind commands the external world, so should intellectual systems master and direct the world's resources through technology. In a democracy resources of mind and will should be able to turn the profit system into an aesthetic instrument. Such is Monroe Stahr's corporate dream: to synthesize pragmatism and rationalism as modes of action and creation into an organizational leadership which, through films, would elevate and extend American sensibility.

[1] F. Scott Fitzgerald, *The Last Tycoon* in *Three Novels* (New York: Charles Scribner's Sons, 1953), p. 97.

Though a rationalist in method, Stahr, like Gatsby and Diver, dreams of a past from which he was excluded and to which he would like to return. He "did his own reasoning without benefit of books—and he had just managed to climb out of a thousand years of Jewry into the late eighteenth century. He could not bear to see it melt away—he cherished the parvenu's passionate loyalty to an imaginary past" (118). What better hope for a Jew emerging from the underground than that an impersonal faculty of mind might put an end to subjugation? For the first time Fitzgerald does not allude to an idealist, romantic tradition where the mind functions against the world; rather, with Stahr he refers to the Enlightenment principle that the mind itself had to be catalyst if the world were to be set in order. In historical terms too it makes sense that Stahr—a twentieth-century explorer who, at his best, tried to civilize the Hollywood frontier—looks backward to the eighteenth century, that turning point when rationalist ideology seemed to have new worlds upon which to graft more perfect human societies.

In the thirties as in the eighteenth century, the organizers of new worlds, whether industries or nations, paid a tithe to power. The enlightened Thomas Jefferson disliked slavery but agreed to found the American nation on such an institution. Monroe Stahr cuts profit margins occasionally—" 'It's time we made a picture that'll lose some money' "—but even so keeps in mind that losing money on a " 'quality picture' " will " 'bring in new customers' " (48). Not new structures, he thinks, but executive leadership will salvage the present corporate system. " 'I'm the unity,' " Stahr declares to explain how pictures get made, and his historical kin are the Romans because " 'I've heard that they never invented things but they knew what to do with them.' " He feels that writers' " 'brains belonged to me—because I know how to use them' " (125). Stahr's position raises a question about the relation, in a democracy, between production and individual personality. Too often organizational genius creates products or structures whose significance has been wrongly taken for granted. In Stahr's case all of his gifts perfect a product which is mediocre to begin with and which appeals only to popular taste and fantasy. To particularize the allusions to the Romans it's as if Stahr were a governor trying to organize the province of Gaul, whereas the real issues are the very existence and purpose of the provinces. Like Lincoln, with whom he is compared, Stahr holds things together through force of personality. When he dies, the industry he commanded, not unlike Lincoln's re-established Union, falls into baser hands and serves more selfish ends. The dilemma explored through Stahr is whether or not magnetic and gifted individuals can elevate a system above its own structures and values. The answer in *The Last Tycoon* being *no*, Fitzgerald implies that the only humane solution is a democratic accommodation between the purposes and systems of production and individual needs, talents, and desire. Revised structures, however, there are none.

Before we know any of these things and while Monroe Stahr is simply a blurred and intimidating figure, Fitzgerald projects through the worshipping eyes of his narrator, Cecilia Brady, a heroic of personality: "He had flown up very high to see, on strong wings, when he was young. And while he was up there he had looked on all the kingdoms, with the kind of eyes that can stare straight into the sun. Beating his wings tenaciously— finally frantically—and keeping on beating them, he had stayed up there longer than most of us, and then, remembering all that he had seen from his great height of how things were, he had settled gradually to earth" (20). Satan, Christ, Daedalus—the description evokes the solitary, detached perceiver. But the common mythic reference point implicates personality in history and society. Resolution comes only when intelligence and will forsake the abstractly heroic duel with the blank powers of the universe in order to join the human race. Such an individual leaves off the isolate quest to share his knowledge and his power with the rest of men. For the twentieth-century entrepreneur as for the mythical Daedalus, creative power flows into historical responsibility. In its cunning creations, intellect must confront the moral problem of good and evil as well as the strategic one of ends and means. This the first Daedalus found out when, after he had designed the labyrinth to protect Cretan society from the Minotaur, King Minos used it for criminal revenge upon innocent Athenians, and ultimately, because Daedalus helped these political prisoners escape, against the artificer himself. Daedalus escaped from his own labyrinth because his mind conceived the possibility of man-made wings, whereas Stahr will die in a plane crash expressive of the imperfections, the unpredictables, in modern technology.

At the same time Stahr possesses some of the hubris of unwise Icarus, yet—the difference reflects the distinction between myth and history—he does try to implement his vision within society's framework. Here flaw and virtue coincide. Because of fierce individualism and paternalism, Stahr accepts the film industry's condition " 'that we have to take people's favorite folklore and dress it up and give it back to them' " (105). But he accepts the premise confident that his leadership will inspire results which qualitatively surpass that condition. Moreover, Fitzgerald's notes make clear that he wanted to show not only Stahr's ability, but also to judge him as a man willing to commit murder to preserve his rank in an industry which simplified reality and glorified the mogul: ". . . I want to show that Stahr left certain harm behind him just as he left good behind him. That some of his reactionary creations such as the Screen Playwrights existed long after his death just as so much of his valuable work survived him" (150).

Even more telling is Fitzgerald's conviction that in addition to entertaining the nation, Hollywood was extending a reductive architecture across both national landscape and national consciousness: "Plane might fall in suburb of Los Angeles. He thinks it was hills, but it's right there—a desolation he helped to create" (158). Industry, environment, culture, and consciousness cannot be separated, even if the leaders of society are too preoccupied with success to unify them in humane totality. Responsibility there is, even if, like Stahr, the modern prince becomes so absorbed in machination that he cannot recognize the shape of his own desolation. Finally, insofar as we can tell from Fitzgerald's notes and sketches, Stahr's tragedy is that in his single-mindedness he allows himself to be dehumanized by the very forces he would ruthlessly bring within the scope of human decency.

2

History in *The Last Tycoon* becomes commensurate to the film industry's own tendency to condensation, burlesque, and pragmatism. Very quickly verification and complexity appear as expendables in this novel's world. "Now that Europe is tumbling down around our ears" (141), the force of the immediate present denies to the past the privilege it enjoyed in *The Great Gatsby* and *Tender Is the Night.* Just as we see Hollywood through its chief executive and pioneer, so we must arrange American history according to a succession of fragmentary allusions to past presidents. Early in the novel a visit to The Hermitage occasions some billboard history by Wylie White, an occasionally sober script-writer: " 'Just in time, Mr. Schwartz,' he said. 'The tour is just starting. Home of Old Hickory—America's tenth president. The victor of New Orleans, opponent of the National Bank, and inventor of the Spoils System' " (12). If Andrew Jackson can be reduced to such banality and venality, then where is Manny Schwartz on the scale of existence? The answer drives that ruined soul to suicide, but not before he says of White and his brash summary: " 'Knows everything and at the same time he knows nothing' " (12). But in the Hollywood writer's "treatment" life and history necessarily become drained of feeling and complexity. These writers' very brains belong to executives who assume that individual creation is impractical, unreliable, unmarketable. The movies are reality; the world around Hollywood has become a set, its human beings extras, life itself a series of interchangable "treatments."

In addition, there is a feeling of relief that the past is dead and unable to unsettle us further. For when Prince Agge, listed in Fitzgerald's sketch as an early Fascist, notices Abraham Lincoln in the studio commissary "sitting here, his legs crossed, his kindly face fixed on a forty-cent dinner, including dessert, his shawl wrapped around him as if to protect himself from the erratic air-cooling," he is moved to sympathetic admiration. Legend has seemingly become flesh exactly according to its word. But all at once the factitious extra asserts himself in unexpected fashion. Unguided by director or legend, "Lincoln suddenly raised a triangle of pie and jammed it in his mouth, and, a little frightened, Prince Agge hurried to join Stahr" (49). We like the past neat and ordered, and if even our recapitulations of history break away from us into the unexpected, the exigent, then how messy, troubled, and insoluble must the past itself have been? Neither is the present neat. Economic chaos, union agitation, threats of war, and, above all for Stahr and many other Hollywood tycoons, the fact that "Jews were dead miserably beyond the sea" (116) appear through the costumes to jar their logical control over reality.

There is in this novel a greater gravity assigned to Lincoln's historical personality. George Boxley, an English novelist who gives only second best to Stahr, for self-protection tries to understand this man's puzzling talent. Finally, with Lincoln his reference point, he sees Stahr and historical leadership in identical terms—pragmatic accomplishment: "He recognized that Stahr like Lincoln was a leader carrying on a long war on many fronts; almost single-handedly he had moved pictures sharply forward through a decade, to a point where the content of the 'A productions' was wider and richer than that of the stage. Stahr was an artist only, as Mr. Lincoln was a general, perforce and as a layman" (106). Both men do what they have to do to be true to the standards they have set for themselves. History's necessities intensify their vitality and quicken what Fitzgerald called in himself "kinetic impulses." [2] Through a coalition of intelligence, will, and a tough sense of timing, Stahr and Lincoln exercise mastery over diverse human talents and personalities. Under pressure they know what to do and can organize others to carry the imperative action. Unfortunately, neither man successfully brings together vision and action in a process both practical and theoretical.

As the presidential allusions grow more contemporary, a call to Stahr, supposedly from Franklin Roosevelt, whom he's talked to before, turns out to be from a man with a talking orangoutang which resembles William McKinley. This, everyone else feels, is as it should be, but Stahr is embarrassed and disappointed because he does not talk to Roosevelt. He seems to cherish an awe of this contemporary president exactly because he is right now wielding power for the sake of coherence in the nation. If the movies' aesthetic reference point is popular taste, the nation's political mode is charisma exercised on behalf of the system. Changes in both orders will be minor—mere concessions to enable the economy to regain its balance.

3

Finally, what is clearest in *The Last Tycoon* is Monroe Stahr, the man. ACTION IS CHARACTER, Fitzgerald insisted in his notes for this novel, and the statement defines the externalizing process crucial to Stahr's personality. For what this book is about is the struggle to abandon illusions and enter into life. In its simple outline the story of Monroe Stahr asserts the incompatibility between a leader's work in the world and any passionate, tender private life. Stahr, the man who would humanize Hollywood's creations—"he submitted the borderline pictures to the

[2] Andrew Turnbull, ed., *The Letters of F. Scott Fitzgerald* (New York: Charles Scribner's Sons, 1963), p. 430.

negro and found them trash" (95)—must himself be humanized and sensitized by intimacy. Indeed, when Stahr and Kathleen make love for the first time, it's a little as if we were back with Gatsby and Daisy in 1917. Tenderness between them follows sexual consummation. First there is an essentially impersonal physical impulse, and then the risk and nakedness of sexuality attracts them to sentiment and curiosity about each other as persons. Unlike Gatsby, Stahr does not idealize Kathleen. As it should, their union separates her from the images of Minna, Stahr's dead wife, images which only another woman could change from fixation to memory.

The old dichotomy is hard to break; for too long has work been love and love been work. Having lived from his mind and will, Stahr finds himself dying; to save himself he must restore vitality to his body. In the same way he must feel and see that sensibility is not merely a stamp to be branded onto films, but an immediate response to all the phenomena of one's life:

> Like many brilliant men, he had grown up dead cold. Beginning at about twelve, probably, with the total rejection common to those of extraordinary mental powers, the "See here: this is all wrong—a mess—all a lie—and a sham—," he swept it all away, everything, as men of his type do; and then instead of being a son-of-a-bitch as most of them are, he looked around at the barrenness that was left and said to himself, "*This* will never do." And so he had learned tolerance, kindness, forbearance, and even affection like lessons (97).

"I think, therefore I am" flows into: "I recite, therefore I am human." But there are human parts which Cartesian perception and methods do not cover. Stahr's life as the modern Machiavellian prince has denied him, even with his wife, the "privilege of giving himself unselfishly to another human being" (139). "Dead cold" himself, in intention more than in fact, until he meets Kathleen Stahr distills his desire into love stories he knows to be synthetic and stereotypic.

In their last meeting, however, Stahr loses Kathleen because of an uncharacteristic failure to act in the confident and arbitrary way that had brought him to power over a cut-throat industry. Again we watch the division of manhood, strong and individual in the world, but weak and prosaic with a woman: " 'Suppose you were a railroad man,' [Stahr] said. 'You have to send a train through there somewhere. Well, you get your surveyors' reports, and you find there's three or four or a half a dozen gaps, and no one is better than the other. You've got to decide—on what basis? You can't test the best way—except by doing it. So you just do it' " (19). For the world's sake, the will creates one certainty from many possibilities. But what of one's own sake? With the woman he loves the executive remains an executive as if private life ran according to the same clock which measures reality in the studio, day after day, year after year—impersonally.

> It was a deep and desperate time-need, a clock ticking with his heart, and it urged him, against the whole logic of his life, to walk past her into the house now and say, "This is forever" . . .

> "We'll go to the mountains tomorrow," said Stahr. Many thousands of people depended on his balanced judgment—you can suddenly blunt a quality you have lived by for twenty years (116).

The same elements of chance and contingency which mind and will convert to active choices in executive situations paralyze Stahr when he faces commitment to human intimacy. When his heart compels him to a new life, he cannot "just do it." The mind's routine will not be altered, not even on the chance of happiness.

Stahr's heart specialist—also a professional man—blames his patient's imminent collapse more on unnatural psychic drives than on any flaw of the heart: "You couldn't persuade a man like Stahr to stop and lie down and look at the sky for six months. He would much rather die. He said differently, but what it added up to was the definite urge toward total exhaustion that he had run into before" (108). Here the body at last becomes a machine incapable of revitalizing itself. Fitzgerald in *The Last Tycoon*'s final complete scene—written the day he died—shows, in Stahr's feeble attack on the Communist Brimmer, how loss of Kathleen has turned insane those energies within Stahr capable of merging tenderness and leadership. Without contact and love, it seems a man must parcel himself out in small perishable pieces until there is nothing left for any action or any relationship. Stahr's tragedy is that he acts as if the legend about himself as irreplaceable executive were all fact and no rhetoric. Desire for power and a sense of responsibility for his culture have led him away from the intimate needs of his personality. The woman he loves—she is the grace, the class, the intimacy denied him by his aggressive drive—is expandable before his executive identity.

Also expendable, in a crisis, are the democratic values he would distill on the screen to the masses. In Monroe Stahr Fitzgerald embodies the failure of a man ambitious for power and desirous of love to humanize his society enough to live in fulfillment himself. The demands and circumstances of power rule out even survival. The novel indicts the tendency to confuse aesthetic values with corporate structure; it testifies to the impossibility of an open-ended individual talent flourishing in the collective enterprise of American capitalism. Fittingly, in a world where people are objects and objects people, Fitzgerald chooses Stahr's briefcase for epitaph, hoping that, as in the movies, its appearance, if not its contents, will motivate the finder toward an honorable course of action. From his sketch it appears Fitzgerald's fears were in danger of realization and that, at least in this novel, form might have rationalized a desolation of vision.

ten

Personality is complexity

Literary criticism begins with observation and ends in judgment: What *is* the relation between form and value, beauty and personality? Nor are these separate categories distinct from one another across the spaces of consciousness. Unified, they embody a critic's conception of humanity. So too Fitzgerald passes a judgment of complexity upon personality through his characters and their encounters with different frameworks of American life and thought. It is the essence of his novels to show the disintegration of men who discover reality to be other than those categorical images imagination had considered absolute in time and space. I refer to the twin categories of women and America. Although each reality defies this conceptual mode, each is a category because both are so perceived and defined by the men whose dreams dominate Fitzgerald's novels.

To Gatsby, to Diver, and to Stahr women are rarely person-alities, rarely individuals, rarely human beings; above all, they are rarely women. Consistently, they assume metaphorical values which reflect the divided allegiance of Fitzgerald's heroes to a romantic transcendence and to a vision of the world as resource to be possessed and held in dominion. In the process metaphor becomes a club (one thinks of the double effect of Prospero's aesthetic vision) instead of a wand whereby the integrity of a particular reality is heightened through its unexpected relation-ship to some other thing or personality. In its truest form meta-

phor brings the perceiver to a full sense of some reality only partially recognized beforehand. Yeats's comparison of the heart to
a foul rag-and-bone shop may shock us into passion or grief, but
finally it leads us to the heart itself—a bloody, beating thing
within our own breast. Those who experience metaphor become
articulators of their own unique and universal experience.
Through style human beings become persons.

But Fitzgerald's American men replace complex human reality
with categorical conceptions. The aesthetic moments of Gatsby,
Diver, and Stahr do not connect beauty and personality to the
world and its complexities of time and history. Daisy is a Dream
Girl, Nicole has no background, Kathleen is Beautiful Doll.
Daisy and Nicole are seen by Gatsby and Diver as embodiments
either of innocence (woman and continent before discovery) or
of corruption (woman and America spoiled by male exploitation) but never as a complex mixture of qualities and values.
Their relationships evade maturity; both through idealism and
cynicism, sentimentality defines love. Metaphor submerges these
women, and the metaphorical structure is dualistic. Gatsby,
Diver, and Stahr perceive women as commodities, sexual embodiments of that America promised every boy by the democratic dream, then either denied by the economic and social
system or fulfilled in a way that diminishes the freedom and
complexity of personality, i.e., tycoon Monroe Stahr.

Gatsby, Diver, and Stahr raise adolescent fantasy to the level
of life's imperative. Internalized, the fantasies replace that
American world to which they are similar but not identical in
the first place.

> A universe of ineffable gaudiness spun itself out in his brain
> while the clock ticked on the wash-stand and the moon soaked
> with wet light his tangled clothes upon the floor. Each night
> he added to the pattern of his fancies until drowsiness closed
> down upon some vivid scene with an oblivious embrace. For a
> while these reveries provided an outlet for his imagination;
> they were a satisfactory hint of the unreality of reality, a promise

that the rock of the world was founded securely on a fairy's wing (*The Great Gatsby*, p. 75).

He sat in the churches as he sat in his father's church in Buffalo, amid the starchy must of Sunday clothes. He listened to the wisdom of the Near East, was Crucified, Died, and was Buried in the cheerful church, and once more worried between five or ten cents for the collection plate, because of the girl who sat in the pew behind (*Tender Is the Night*, p. 211).

Her talk of kings had carried him oddly back in flashes to the pearly White Way of Main Street in Erie, Pennsylvania, when he was fifteen. There was a restaurant with lobsters in the window and green weeds and bright lights on a shell cavern, and beyond behind a red curtain the terribly strange brooding mystery of people and violin music. That was just before he left for New York. This girl reminded him of the fresh iced fish and lobsters in the window. She was Beautiful Doll (*The Last Tycoon*, p. 114).

Insofar as women become identified with America in these men's minds, their aesthetic and sexual qualities become social and economic; women, that is, become to the male imagination mere projections of class and wealth. In the paradigm male identity depends upon acceptance not so much by an individual woman as by a masculine structure of wealth and privilege. Women, therefore, are not women; they are commodities obtained by those who have mastered the system.

This psychology of private life may derive from earliest American values which derived from an eighteenth-century rationalist view of personality and society. *We hold these truths to be self-evident, that all men are created equal, that they are endowed by their Creator with certain inalienable Rights, that among these are Life, Liberty and the pursuit of Happiness.* The Declaration of Independence flowed from an Enlightenment context, its God-given rights those natural rights defined by John Locke as life, liberty, and estate or property. Or did it, completely? Was the change made by Jefferson, Franklin, and the others one of substance and policy or of euphemism and image? By itself pursuit of happiness asserts diversity as a first principle of national life. In fact, under the structures of the eighteenth century (and nineteenth and twentieth), the phrase was ignored and contradicted by practical policies.

What if we were to read Fitzgerald's novels as a paradigm of the struggle between property and the pursuit of happiness in American history and consciousness? What did the new phrase promise if not that life and liberty would be interpreted humanely and democratically? Historically, however, the values belonging to pursuit of happiness were so oriented around wealth and property, money and capital, that men found even their desires for love and beauty expressed in a mode of possession. Gatsby and Diver in fiction, Jefferson and Wilson in history, believed that in America a man could choose a life of aesthetic reality and humane vision. Whatever the grip of property on this nation, the phrase "pursuit of happiness" remained an open-ended promise that beckoned individuals in succeeding generations to forget facts and policies and remember a euphemism which even in the beginning stood for an old order while promising democratic policies. Instead of recognizing the language as fraudulent because of context and policy—if all men were equal why was a black slave's child the property of his white master and why did a federal anti-lynch law fail to pass the United States Senate as late as the 1930's? Men verified their dreams by trying to transcend language and history.

In reality pursuit of happiness and property referred to the same vision: in America power has been the establishment of wealth, and success the measure of one's contributions to an imperial system. Gatsby's re-creation of himself was in the platonic mode all right, but the ideal forms were ungraspable, elite though material. Mere images make certain that only the illusions of wealth and power will be extended to the majority of citizens. Complexity denied, transcendence chosen over history, the idealist's psychology explicitly denies the pull of property and possession only to find, like Gatsby, that the American ideal was no more and no less than a romantic image of material prosperity.

Nevertheless there remains in America a tension between pursuit of happiness and property as values. Fitzgerald shows how idealism, when dependent upon a desire to be admired and accepted by those in power, is subverted and paralyzed by the actual conditions and values of America because these very values have been cherished in secret by the idealists themselves. Found out first by the world and then by themselves, they have no identity left for self-reconstruction; they judge neither themselves nor the world worthy of commitment and action.

Let aesthetic contemplation stand for a person's best relation to others and the world. The meaning of Fitzgerald's novels is that the aesthetic impulse has got to be continuous and not just a moment in opposition to the rest of life. There must be a commitment to otherness and to that harmony dependent upon connecting oneself to the world. The process of defining women more as symbols than as persons removes the male imagination from the complexity of human contact. Such men annihilate their own personalities; they become invisible to the world and to themselves. By itself, no thing or no one exists dynamically and in harmony. When resilient and diverse, human contact can reverberate in achievements that create a culture whose integrity is simultaneously particular and universal.

"I am not a great man," Fitzgerald wrote before his death, "but, sometimes I think the impersonal and objective quality of my talent and the sacrifices of it, in pieces, to preserve its essential value has some sort of epic grandeur." [1] The essential, about himself, about his wife and child, about his talent and his nation, commanded his loyalty. To the end his compassionate imagination sought a dialectic which could integrate history and self— and change both—through the social form of the novel. For all

[1] Andrew Turnbull, ed., *The Letters of F. Scott Fitzgerald* (New York: Charles Scribner's Sons, 1963), p. 62.

their pain and loss his novels with their moral sympathy and historical intelligence put contemporary Americans in touch with ourselves and maybe even move us toward a society whose values, language, and policies will harmonize in democratic forms.

Index

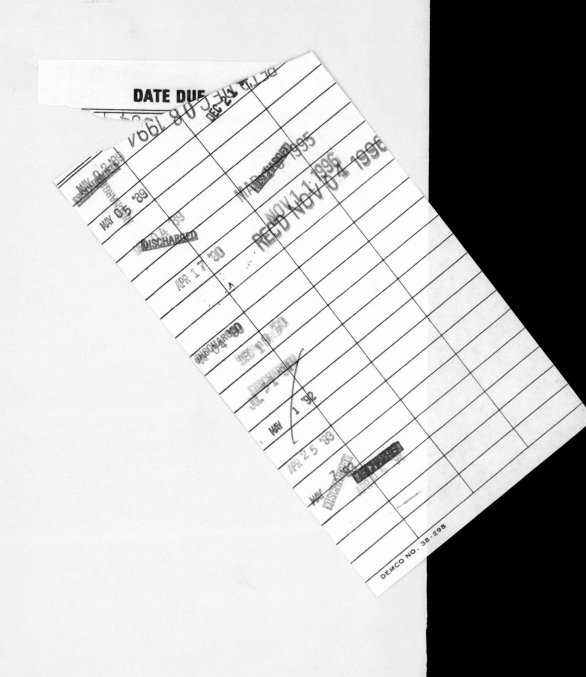

DATE DUE

DEMCO NO. 38-298